'Challenging, thought-prov... biblical, moving, full
of hope and insp...

Rob P... ...ily

'Challenging, thought-provoking, at times
heartbreaking. This is no ordinary book. This is
Krish and Miriam calling the Church to action. They
have lived the book and now we are invited to share
in their passion. If taken seriously, the impact not
only on thousands of vulnerable children and teenagers, but on us as a country, will be immeasurable.'
Steve Clifford, General Director, Evangelical Alliance UK

'Scripture reminds us that love never fails. Indeed
loving the marginalised and vulnerable is the
Church's mandate. And this thoroughly brilliant
book, which resonates with God's heart for the
orphan, is, in my opinion, an essential, practical
guide. I beseech you to read it, be inspired by it, and
then act on it. In fact I defy anyone to reach the last
pages of *Home for Good* and not feel compelled to
help a "forgotten" child in need of a family.'
*Diane Louise Jordan, television and radio presenter,
inspirational speaker and author*

'Krish and Miriam Kandiah write from a deep well of
experience as they explore the landscape of adoption
and fostering in today's culture. In this book they

provide practical models to help anyone who has a vision to offer homes to some of the most vulnerable in our society.'
Revd Nicky Gumbel, Holy Trinity Brompton

'The story of God is a narrative of adoption into his family the Church. Adoption, in its broadest sense, is what we were saved for and what we are saved to do! Krish Kandiah outlines the thrilling possibilities for today's Christians in adoption and fostering, bringing the weight of first-hand experience to important, practical questions. I commend his message wholeheartedly to church leaders and to Christian families throughout the land.'
Pete Greig, 24–7 Prayer, Alpha International and Emmaus Road Church

'Full of evocative stories that remind us of our own adoption into the family of God, this book will move and inspire you to find ways to protect and care for the most vulnerable in our society. With 50,000 children currently on the child protection register and more being added daily, Krish and Miriam raise some provocative questions that need urgent answers, including: could we individually find space in our hearts and our homes for these children and could the Church collectively respond to this crisis to give these young people hope and a better future?'
Patrick Regan OBE, Founder and CEO of XLP

'Wholehearted discipleship to Jesus Christ most always intertwines both joy and sorrow, great cost and great reward. Perhaps nowhere is this more true than as Christians reflect the way God first loved us as they open their hearts and homes to the fatherless. *Home for Good* invites us deep into this unparalleled journey, weaving together a soaring vision with gritty truths and hard-earned wisdom.'
Jedd Medefind, President, Christian Alliance for Orphans

'Krish and Miriam Kandiah have served the Church extremely well with this book, not just in the UK, but in the whole English-speaking world. They have beautifully and compellingly woven together the theology of adoption and its practice for the great good of vulnerable children. What I love most about *Home for Good* is that it empowers us to care for the vulnerable by making much of God's grace to us in Jesus.'
Dan Cruver, Founder of Together for Adoption; author of Reclaiming Adoption

'Let me just say that this is an extraordinarily powerful text – I've never before done a theological editing job (and I've done a few . . .) which has left my keyboard wet with tears because the book was so moving.'
Steve Holmes, Senior Lecturer in Theology, University of St Andrews

'Krish and Miriam's book forces us to face up to the plight of many vulnerable children in our society. I stand with them in their plea to all Christians and the Church to respond to our calling to be salt and light in this particular darkness. I have spent my whole professional life working with and for vulnerable citizens and I wholeheartedly commend this book to you.'
Professor Keith Brown, Director, National Centre for Post Qualifying Social Work, Bournemouth University

'This is the book I would say the Church and vulnerable children in the UK have been waiting for, no less than that. The pages exude honesty, love, compassion and an entirely appropriate theological challenge to care for orphans.'
Revd Sue Colman, adoptee, Radical Hospitality Project Manager (William Wilberforce Trust)

'Fostering and adoption is a vital issue that the Church must engage with. This book provokes us to put our faith into action and inspires us to do something for the children affected by these issues. Whether through becoming a carer or an advocate for children who are in the care system, ultimately this book will help you on your journey to live out your Christian faith.'
Revd Yemi Adedeji, Global Ambassador for Compassion and One People Commission Director, Evangelical Alliance

HOME FOR GOOD

MAKING A DIFFERENCE FOR VULNERABLE CHILDREN

KRISH KANDIAH WITH
MIRIAM KANDIAH

HODDER &
STOUGHTON

First published in Great Britain in 2013 by Hodder & Stoughton
An Hachette UK company

This reissue first published in 2019

1

The stories in this book are true. Names and some minor details have been changed
to protect confidentiality.

A CIP catalogue record for this title is available from the British Library

ISBN 978 1 529 35529 1
eBook ISBN 978 1 444 74532 0

Typeset in Chaparral MM by Palimpsest Book Production Limited, Falkirk,
Stirlingshire
Printed and bound in Great Britain by Clays Ltd, Elcograf S.p.A.

Hodder & Stoughton policy is to use papers that are natural, renewable and
recyclable products and made from wood grown in sustainable forests. The logging
and manufacturing processes are expected to conform to the environmental
regulations of the country of origin.

Hodder & Stoughton Ltd
Carmelite House
50 Victoria Embankme
London EC4Y 0DZ

www.hodderfaith.com

CONTENTS

Preface   ix

Foreword by Rob Parsons   xiii

Introduction: What do you care?!   1

1   Why something must be done and why we must do something   12

2   Why kids end up in care and where kids in care end up   28

3   Why vulnerable people are best placed to help vulnerable children   41

4   Why children need homes, not children's homes   55

5   Why relieving suffering means receiving suffering   70

6   Why caring about worship means worship by caring   91

7   Why we are called to hold on and let go   108

8   Why adopting a Jesus model affects why we adopt   126

9   Why we hope to turn fear into hope   144

10   Why hard-to-place children can find a home for good   164

11 What next?   179

Afterword   182

Acknowledgements   184

Notes   187

PREFACE

Since my wife and I wrote this book five years ago, many readers have suggested that it was missing a health warning. They say that someone should have let them know before they even got to chapter one that this book would not only inform them, or perhaps inspire them, but may impact their life to such an extent that it would never be the same again.

So here it is: a warning before you turn any more pages.

Recently I met a church pastor who was keen to introduce me to his wife and two daughters. He told me that he had been at the same Christian summer festival as me (and 35,000 young people) years earlier when I had hosted a seminar about fostering and adoption. Despite not actually attending the seminar, something made both him and his wife choose this book for their holiday reading; by the time they took the flight home, they knew that God was calling them to start their family through adoption. Both had been challenged by the knowledge that mixed race children in sibling groups are some of the children who wait the longest to find adoptive families, and so here, smiling up at me, were two sisters thriving in the loving care of this couple, with the support of their whole church community.

I could have cried with joy. Again. Because over the past five years as I have travelled the length and breadth of the UK – even as far away as Singapore and Australia – I have had the privilege of meeting family after family with similar stories. Each one affirms the vision I was given when I first began fostering: those of us who know what it is to be adopted into God's family are best placed to help the children in our care system who are waiting for loving homes.

Something else has changed since this book was first published. The namesake campaign that it launched has now become a fully-fledged charity that continues to equip the UK Church to respond to the needs of vulnerable children. We journey with hundreds of people each year as they go from the point of inspiration, to welcoming children into their home, and we resource churches in every part of the UK to be safe and supportive communities for every family who cares. As Founding Director I have the privilege of leading Home for Good into places that we couldn't have imagined five years ago, including Westminster, Stormont and Holyrood and multiple visits to Downing Street, as we advocate for vulnerable children and the families who care for them. Our vision remains the same as it was when we began: to provide a home for every child who needs one.

As you read this book you will discover a biblical case for why adoption and foster care are a much-needed expression of Christian worship in our world right now. You will also come across amazing stories of ordinary Christians doing extraordinary things to help vulnerable children. These are active ingredients – the Holy Spirit-inspired word of God and the Holy Spirit-empowered people of God living out their faith. I warn you now this is a powerful combination and may lead you to face up to a new challenge to your life and faith.

One businessman I know started the process to foster immediately after reading this book. He also bought fifteen copies to give away to his friends because he wanted them to know why he was doing it and how they could help him on this new adventure. He understood that not everyone is called to foster or adopt, but every Christian is called to demonstrate the radical love of God to those who are most in need.

Are you prepared to go on a journey that is leading an ever-increasing number of people to radically disrupt their lives for the sake of vulnerable children? I am not promising easy reading – it is certainly not an easy calling – but when did Jesus ever say that following him would be easy? My prayer as you read this book is that you will join the growing movement of people around the world that will do whatever it takes to make sure that every child that needs one has a home for good.

There. Don't say you haven't been warned. Read on at your own risk.

Krish Kandiah
April 2019

FOREWORD

Sometimes when you read a book you will have a glimpse of something that you believe reveals part of the Father heart of God. This happened to me when I was fortunate to be asked to read the manuscript of Krish and Miriam Kandiah's new book. It is both challenging and thought-provoking, and always brings us back to a biblical perspective. Although my wife Dianne and I have never adopted or fostered a child, I remember well the day that a young man arrived to share our home. It was on a Christmas Eve and he rang our doorbell. Dianne opened the door and there was Ronnie, clutching a chicken and saying, 'Can I join you for Christmas dinner?'

That was nearly forty years ago. Up to that point, Ronnie had spent most of his life in a care home. We invited him in to stay the night with us, and somehow one day turned into two, and then three. He never left. When he came we hadn't been married long and didn't have children, but today our kids are grown, have left home and have children of their own . . . and Ronnie is still with us.

Soon after he began to live with us, Dianne discovered that many of the things we took for granted about family life, Ronnie had little or no experience of. The staff of the care homes he had lived in had tried hard to produce a home-like environment, but it just wasn't the same. So things that we took for granted, like birthdays, anniversaries or a simple family get-together, were totally new experiences for him, and in many ways he was discovering a whole new meaning of the word 'family'!

There are still many children in our nation today in desperate need of a family. Many of them, like Ronnie, have no or only poor family experiences to look back on. In the UK a child comes into the care system every fifteen minutes.

In many ways I believe they are the 'forgotten ones'. In this book, Krish and Miriam have done us a wonderful service in weaving together two strands: they give us a window into the world of hurting, scared children, who just want to be part of a family, and they also open up to us more understanding of God's heart for each one of us.

Maybe some of us have forgotten that once we were 'not a people', until God called us out of darkness into his wonderful light. Now we are the people of God, adopted as his sons and daughters, and God is calling us to show the same love and acceptance to those who are on the margins. Many of today's 'looked after' children are crying out for the feeling of love and acceptance that God has shown to us.

This book doesn't gloss over the challenges of caring for these children, but at the same time it lifts our eyes to see that when we respond to that calling, we are expressing the heartbeat of God. It shines new light on familiar

Scriptures in a way that will refresh your spirit and challenge you to consider new perspectives. I found it a
humbling and inspiring read. Krish and Miriam have
'walked the walk', and their passion for children and their
passion for God shine through. It is a moving book, full of
hope and inspiration.

I am full of admiration for those who make room in
their homes and hearts for the vulnerable. I know that
those who have accepted the challenge of adopting,
fostering or caring for a child in need have no wish to be
put on a pedestal and admired from afar. And they don't
want our pity or sympathy. But they do need our support,
and they need us to consider getting involved in one of
this nation's most pressing issues. This isn't just for super-
heroes; all of us can and should ask ourselves what God
would have us do.

I really believe that everyone in our churches should hear
this message. Read this book if you are involved in caring
for children in need, and be encouraged. And read this book
if you want to be closer to God and understand his heart;
read it thoughtfully, and read it to be challenged. Let it
shape your thinking and stir your soul.

Rob Parsons
Chairman and CEO of Care for the Family

INTRODUCTION

WHAT DO YOU CARE?!

Four strangers, three minutes, two police officers and one missing person's report. Talk about a strange weekend.

One wintry Friday night several years ago a girl stood in our hallway. At least, they told us she was a girl. Wearing an oversized unisex tracksuit and trainers, she held her head low, ensuring that her hoody covered her eyes. Her hands never left her pockets and her mouth was muffled in a scarf. All we could see of her was the tip of her nose.

The social worker explained that our house was a safe home where she could stay for a couple of nights, promising that first thing on Monday morning we could all discuss together a longer-term solution.

Before the social worker had even finished introducing us, the 12-year-old blurted out, 'What do you care?!' and exercised her right to walk out of the house unrestrained, disappearing into the night.

'What do you care?!'

There was no chance to answer.

To be honest, we felt kind of relieved. We only had experience parenting babies and younger kids, and were pretty clueless at the time as to the sort of issues we would have had to face if she had stayed. We felt totally ill-equipped and unsuitable for this placement.

As instructed by the social worker, we spent an hour or two looking for her, then called the police to report her as officially missing. The squad car pulled up and two six-foot uniformed officers complete with handcuffs, vests and utility belts squeezed into our lounge to file their report. 'Description of missing person?' they asked. Apart from the pinkish colour of her nose, their question had us pretty much stumped.

We had other questions too.

What was she running from? What had happened to her that she couldn't trust that we would care for her? Why couldn't she run home? Where would a 12-year-old feel safe on the streets of the city?

Lots of questions. No answers.

'What do you care?!'

When the Hoody Kid walked out of the house, her question decided to hang around a while longer.

That question was still nagging at us at church on Sunday morning. It happened that we worshipped at the school she attended. To our surprise, scribbled up on the staff-room wall was her full name followed by details of an incident she had been involved in during the week.

For the next few months we couldn't walk into church

without her name staring us in the face. Invariably it was closely coupled with a word like WARNING, DETENTION, SUSPENDED and, eventually, EXPELLED.

It was distracting. We were supposed to be concentrating on the sermon or joining in the singing.

Imagine trying to worship God with a teenager's sullen and hopeless accusation 'What do you care?!' ringing around your head.

This had a massive impact on us.

First of all, we began to recognise that the Hoody Kid's challenge was not a distraction from worship, but rather a God-given drive to worship. The more we read the Bible, the more we heard God's clear message: if you care about worship, you should worship by caring.

The Bible is full of calls to God's people to worship him through caring for the excluded, the poor and the vulnerable, and especially for children caught up in those circumstances. There are at least forty times where the Bible refers specifically to God's concern for the orphans or the 'fatherless'. That's more than the number of times Scripture talks about tithing or taking communion. It's time to rethink our priorities.

Secondly, the Hoody Kid's question challenged us to move beyond saying we care to actually showing we care. Seeking to develop a godly attitude of compassion from the comfort of our pews is a far cry from really working out how practically we could be active in showing God's compassion in the clutter of messed-up lives.

We live in a broken world, where UNICEF currently identifies 17.6 million orphans, many of them under the impression that nobody really cares about them.[1] Some of these children are in our own communities and towns. A minority of them experience something of God's kindness and compassion through the ministry of Christian teachers, social workers, police officers, foster and adoptive parents, medics, exclusion counsellors, friends and neighbours, showing kids coming into care in whatever ways they can the truth that they are loved, valued and cared for. We would love to see these ministries recognised, supported and encouraged in our local churches, so that others can catch a vision for them too.

Thirdly, the Hoody Kid's plight highlighted on that white board at the back of our church gathering Sunday after Sunday sparked an idea. What if the whole Church began to take her challenge seriously? What if Christians worshipped by caring for the children in the care system? What if Christians could be part of a campaign that brought fostering and adoption ministries back into the heart of the Church in our nation? What if we the Church could be known as the people who truly care about the pain and problems of children who have no other family to turn to and whom, it seems, nobody wants? What if the Church was known as the most compassionate and hospitable family in the country?

There are more kids in care in the UK than there have ever been before. More than 60 per cent of these children have been removed from their homes because of known neglect or abuse.[2] There are suffering, scarred and damaged children living right round the corner from you. What if your church could be the community of hope and healing for these children?

All of us are broken and damaged in one way or another and yet God did not turn a blind eye or turn his back on us. It was costly, but he made a way to take us in. He showed us unconditional love. He gave us hope and a chance to start again. He gave us a family. God gave us a home for good with him forever.

Every Christian's story is the story of an adoption and the story of a home for good with God.

Therefore Christians are uniquely placed to reach out to children in care because once we needed adopting too. Because we understand the sense of identity, belonging, family and purpose that comes from knowing we have a home for good, we want to make sure other people get to experience that too, especially the most vulnerable and broken people in our communities.

This book will address these three aspects of the Hoody Kid's challenge.

To what extent are we as individuals in tune with God's heart for the vulnerable that pulses through every book of the Bible?

Where are the opportunities for us as individuals and families to put into practice the compassion of God by meeting the needs of vulnerable children in our communities?

What would happen if we as the Church rediscovered

our own adoption story and took seriously our adoption mandate?

We shall see together that the Bible teaches us that this involvement in the lives of the vulnerable is a critical element of our worship, an essential part of our obedience, an integral aspect of our mission, a vital way in which we mirror God's character to a watching world, and a visible metaphor of God's love for us.

This book unashamedly asks you to pass on the blessings you have received as adopted children of God and consider stepping forward and getting involved in the lives of children who need your care, your wisdom, your experience, your voice, your attention, your friendship, your love, and maybe even a place in your home.

Some of you will be inspired to offer a child or children waiting for adoption a home for good, a forever family where they are loved unconditionally and nurtured and encouraged to reach their potential.

Some of you will be inspired to use your home for the good of children in need of foster care. A temporary stopgap where wounds can be lovingly tended to, trust and self-esteem can begin to be rebuilt and the healing process can get started.

Some of you will be inspired to help make your churches a spiritual home for good for kids from difficult home backgrounds. A place of welcome. A place of inclusion. A family unlike any other that embraces and protects vulnerable children, and offers them healing and hope.

Whoever you are, there is a role for you to play in the whole ministry of adoption, fostering and orphan care. This book is for the whole Church, because it takes a whole church to capture the vision and work it out in our homes and communities.

As both foster and adoptive parents ourselves we know we couldn't do it without the whole church sharing the vision and working together.

We couldn't make our family a home for good without:

- those long-standing friends in the church who know us well enough to write honest references, enabling our local authority to assess our suitability to help the children they see coming into care;
- those members of the church who smile at our children, take time to make them feel special, care for them, pray for them, look out for them, and get to know their names and their needs;
- those parents in the church who allow their children to befriend our foster children, not knowing whether that friendship will last days, weeks, months or years, or how they will eventually explain to their own children why they had to move on;
- those professionals in the church who help us know how to go about looking for solutions to medical, behavioural, educational or legal issues;
- the other adopters and foster carers in the church who understand the problems and processes and can

offer a listening ear, advice, prayer and a shoulder to lean on;

- the respite carers in the church who have stepped in offering up their homes for as long as is needed in an emergency, enabling consistency of care for children when we have been unable to be there for them;
- the leaders in the church who faithfully serve us, even though as a family we are rather unconventional and unpredictable;
- the network of friends of friends in the church who can source the strangest things at short notice, whether it is a baby's stroller or a pair of wellies or a costume for a school play.

Thank you to this wonderful team who partner with us, support us and encourage us to keep going. You are the inspiration behind this book. We love worshipping God with you.

And thank you to all the children whom we have had the privilege of parenting over the years, wherever you are now. You have taught us so much. We love you and miss you.

Reader, whatever your family situation, whatever your level of faith, whatever your workload, whatever your gifts and talents, God has got a place for you to join in this mission that is close to his heart and incredibly rewarding.

ASHLEY'S STORY

I went into care at the age of two. I had a fragmented upbringing with a whole load of different people. Being in care was normal for me. I moved around a lot and I became desensitised to change, abandonment and rejection.

My first foster mum was a wonderful typical Jamaican woman called Sissy. I loved her. I still have happy memories of kicking a football in her garden. But then one day I was told I had to leave her home. I was given no adequate reason. I didn't really understand what was going on. I was given just a week's warning. I tore up the social worker's papers and I pretended I was going to commit suicide. My whole world crumbled. I felt abandoned.

I vividly remember the day I left Sissy. I woke up, CBeebies was on television and the house was filled with Sissy's cooking and the normal smells of a normal day. I remember a car coming, three strangers arriving and I was taken away to a children's home. My last memory of Sissy was watching her crying as the car pulled away. It was devastating, heartbreaking, tough.

The children's home had ten other lads my age, as well as some shift workers and I stayed there until I was twelve, when I was moved to a family. It was around this time that I began to recognise the deficiencies that I had, the things I lacked at an emotional level. It was also around this time that I saw a dad playing with his child and asked God to be a Father to me. From that moment on I considered the church to be my main family.

I moved again aged fifteen, this time to a brilliant foster mum and a foster dad, with a studious sister and a good family structure. Moving about so much I got used to having transient and fleeting relationships. I appreciate so much about the people who cared for me, and I know that what happened to me has made me who I am, but if an adoptive family had come forward early on – one family who would have loved me – then I wouldn't have had the struggles that I have had. The biggest thing I have lacked in my life was just someone to call mum or dad, or preferably both mum and dad.

Since leaving the X Factor 2011 band, The Risk, I have tried to help other children in the care system. I presented a television documentary on fostering, during which I spoke to many good families who felt they did not have the confidence to look after other people's children. But if they could provide love, a meal on the table and a bed in their home, they are good candidates to help, in my opinion. Everybody needs a family to provide love, security and a foundation for life.

Ashley John-Baptiste is a journalist and an advocate for care experienced children and young people.

CHAPTER 1

WHY SOMETHING MUST BE DONE
AND WHY WE MUST DO SOMETHING

We shivered on this unusually cold night in Tirana, Albania. In subsequent years we would realise that every November the sultry Mediterranean summer weather would abruptly vanish and be replaced for four long months by its evil twin – the bitter cold snap that required us to power up the old oil burners and go to bed at sundown under layers of thick woollen blankets. That night, with the chill in the air, we walked home a bit faster than usual. Then something on the pavement caught our eye. What was that? A tiny baby, no more than a few weeks old, swaddled in a blanket lying silently on the street. Some other passers-by dropped a few coins in the bowl alongside the strangely unstirring bundle, and then they disappeared into the darkness.

We did nothing.

We saw her and literally walked by on the other side of the road.

All the way home and half the night we talked about what we should have done. What we could have done for our street-baby.

If we had dropped coins in, the eagle-eyed hustler around the corner would have pocketed the cash for his breakfast, and put his star earner out on the street again the next night. If we had scooped the baby up and brought her home we would have faced the back of the hustler's fist, or the inside of a prison cell for kidnap and sabotage.

If we had come to some arrangement . . . If we had phoned the police . . . If we had access to the Court of Human Rights . . . If we had summoned angels . . .

We talked a lot, but we did nothing.

Married for just over a year, we had often talked about the possibility of adopting. We had both been moved in the past by others' stories of helping children with no family. We had promised to make a difference. But what could we do?

We prayed. We read about God's concern for the poor. We complained about the injustice. We felt bad. But we did nothing.

It was not the first time we had been faced with a need and done nothing. It was not the last. Over the following three years we lived in Tirana we witnessed many babies and young children begging in the city. But that first occasion was and still is one of the most sickening. Our street-baby should be sixteen now. We often wonder what happened to her.

Most of us face a similar dilemma. We know something of the plight of the millions of suffering children around the world who need families. We know something must be done. But we don't really know what we should do, and so we do nothing.

Sometimes when the subject is raised in discussion, we realise this problem has us stumped and so we look for a quick exit. When we introduce our family to people, the subject of fostering and adoption tends to come up, and we are invariably met with one of two hasty and nervous responses.

'Oh, I've always wanted to foster or adopt. The advertising often catches my eye, and I think it would be a great thing to do. It's just I've never got round to making that phone call.'

Or, 'Oh, I could never foster or adopt. My husband/wife isn't around enough. My kids aren't old enough. My house isn't big enough. My work isn't flexible enough. My bank account isn't healthy enough . . .'

The two responses may seem like opposite gut reactions, but perhaps both types of people are in the same boat. Have either really thought about what they could realistically offer? To what extent are they making excuses for doing nothing?

Of course we don't usually say this to their faces. And there may well be legitimate reasons for their concerns. So we put it like this: 'Imagine a car veers off the road and injures me right now, and an ambulance whisks me away to the nearest Accident and Emergency. Would you leave my five helpless children standing here in the street?'

They are outraged. Of course not. They tell us how they would take them home, give them some food, reassure them that they will be taken care of, and then either give them a bed for as long as necessary or arrange some suitable accommodation with a neighbour or friend. We can almost see the mental cogs whirring as they try to find solutions to the logistical issues of mattresses and clothes and schools and car booster seats.

Faced with our hypothetical but specific and quite extreme need, the obstacles and excuses seem to evaporate. Instead of worrying about the process or the cost or the personal inconvenience, most people are keen to get involved, either out of concern for us, as their friends, or out of concern for the children who are standing in front of them distressed.

The relationship is the key. Even people who can manage to walk past a stranger in need will usually jump to help a friend.

Now imagine God was the one who was our friend, and the children in our communities made equal and significant in his image were the ones who are standing in front of us distressed without their parents. Would we do something? If we say we have a relationship with the Creator God we call our Father, Saviour, Lord and friend, shouldn't what matters to him matter to us? If his loved ones need help then shouldn't we jump to do what we can to relieve the vulnerable in their distress?

In this stark verse in James we are told:

> Religion that God our Father accepts as pure and fault-less is this: to look after orphans and widows in their distress. (James 1:27)

This is no obscure instruction, tucked away in a minor letter at the end of our Bibles. This is a clear statement of what God expects of his worshippers, and a summary of what he has been saying throughout history. Caring for widows and orphans is a constantly recurring theme in the Bible that is made explicit even as early as Exodus. In Hebrew, the word orphan referred to any child who had lost their father, irrespective of whether the child's mother was living or not. In a male-dominated society where fathers were the chief providers and protectors, 'to be fatherless meant vulnerability to poverty and disenfranchisement'.[1]

Children in need of fostering (a temporary home when their birth family is in crisis) and adoption (a permanent home as a full family member when their birth family is unable to care for them) are rarely orphans in the strict sense of the word. The term 'vulnerable children' is therefore a closer contemporary equivalent of the Hebrew term orphan. Whether this is vulnerability to risk of poverty, or risk of abuse and neglect, it is precisely these children that we are called over and over throughout Scripture to protect. It is these children that we will be considering how we as individuals, families and the church can help.

This is not to say that caring for vulnerable children is more important than caring for widows. We are to look out for all those who are particularly vulnerable in our world, whether the homeless, the destitute, refugees, the elderly, people with disabilities, those who are trafficked or persecuted, or victims of natural disasters. The list could go on.

But in the UK at the moment there is a crisis in a care system bursting at the seams, which requires our urgent attention.

For a start there are over fifty thousand children on child protection registers. These are the children whom social workers have identified as at continuing risk of physical, emotional or sexual abuse or neglect. But this may be the tip of the iceberg. The National Society for the Prevention of Cruelty to Children (NSPCC) comments that 'Child protection plans are not a measure of the incidence of maltreatment but do give some indication of the scale of the problem by providing figures for the number of children who are judged to be at risk of significant harm. However, research indicates that abuse and neglect are both under-reported and under-recorded.'[2]

There has also been a very large increase in the number of children coming into care. Across the UK more than a hundred children enter the care system every fifteen minutes.[3] Finding suitable homes for these children at this rate is no easy task. According to the charity Fostering

Network, more than eight thousand new foster carers are needed to cope with the increasing demand.[4]

There are also around three thousand children waiting to be adopted, with at least a quarter of children waiting more than a year for an adoptive family. At least half of the children waiting are in sibling groups, and many will have additional or complex needs, or developmental uncertainty.

Behind these statistics there are real children shivering and starving and being exploited on the streets of our own towns and cities in this country. There are kids hidden away in homes near us being abused and neglected in secret. There are children in our communities whose parents are too ill or incapacitated to take care of them. There are a lot of children in distress today waiting for someone to step in and help them where they are, perhaps even take them home for good.

What can we do?

I was a student when reports came in during 1991 about the horrific genocide in Rwanda. In just a hundred days a million civilians were slaughtered. I felt angry and shocked that neighbours could suddenly turn against each other and use machetes to butcher one another to death. But I was also shocked that thousands of United Nations Peace Keepers stationed there, armed with machine guns and armoured personnel carriers, stood by and watched while the tragedy unravelled before their eyes. They had no mandate and so they took no action.

We don't need to sit back and watch the crisis in our

own country unfold, wondering whether or not to intervene. We have this clear mandate from God:

> Religion that God our Father accepts as pure and fault-
> less is this: to look after orphans and widows in their
> distress. (James 1:27)

This key verse about acceptable worship and practical action
for the sake of the vulnerable follows James' caricature of
a Christian worshipper suffering from a form of spiritual
amnesia. He helps us to imagine someone who sees themselves in a mirror and then instantly forgets what they look
like. Imagine catching your reflection and noting that your
face is still smeared with toothpaste, egg from breakfast,
and bicycle oil, but then deciding not to do anything about
it then walking out of the house for that crucial work
appointment.

The mirror check was a futile exercise. James says it's a
bit like reading God's word, hearing its challenge and then
doing nothing about it.

Reading God's word is pointless if we don't do something
about what we have learned, and if we don't do something
about the children who are being abandoned and abused
around us.

James was not writing this to rich and lazy Christians,
who had nothing better to do than sit and stare at their
own reflection.

No, this letter was written to financially stretched

Christians who were being oppressed by some rich land-owners. If ever there was a group of believers who could feel hard done by, under pressure and in need of a break, it was this church.

In my mind, they could have had a pretty watertight case for ignoring the cold and hungry child exposed to the elements on the cold street in Skenderbeg Square, Tirana: 'Those rich landowners down the road, they have spare rooms and plenty of food to go round and connections in high places – they should tackle the bureaucracy and take the child in. We have enough mouths to feed on our limited rations.'

If the Christians James was writing to have no excuse to ignore the needs of vulnerable children, then we have no excuse either.

I have heard a lot of arguments about why people would or should not get involved in ministering to the poor and vulnerable.

It's not my gift. I'm too busy. I want to focus on evangelism not social transformation. I believe God wants us to reach out to people who are similar to ourselves. We need to pri-oritise the needs of our own church family. We need to think strategically and aim at families who could fund ministries. I don't want to put my family at risk. Deprivation is a long-term problem. Let's focus on quick wins instead. Poor, what poor?

James wouldn't let us get away with any of this.

James writes a hard-hitting letter that doesn't pull its

punches. What the militant atheist Richard Dawkins has been arguing for the past decade or so, James already told us two thousand years ago: Christians are (often) deluded.

What if all our excuses are really a front for our own deliberate or inadvertent self-deception? Knowing and reading our Bibles isn't the answer here, for James specifically challenges us not on biblical knowledge but on biblical obedience.

Many of us are blessed to have a lot of very good Bible teachers in our churches who clearly and consistently expound Scripture. If we have questions about the Bible, we are spoilt for choice for websites, books, smart phone apps and people to help us. There are a lot of incredibly well-taught Christians who sacrifice time and effort each week to pass on what they have learned in Bible study groups and home groups.

If your church is strong on Bible teaching, be grateful. But also be careful.

James warns us that good teaching is not sufficient. It is possible to be very well taught and yet utterly deficient in our worship because the teaching makes no practical difference to the way we live.

According to James, our faith should impact our personal holiness, our thought life, the way we read Scripture, the way we speak to others, and the way we actively care for the vulnerable.

Having grown up in the Church, Jason had heard

James 1:27 being preached on countless occasions. It came in Sunday services, chapel messages and Bible classes. And he had been exposed to the large number of Old Testament texts that explicitly delineate God the Father's care for the widow and the fatherless. But for the better part of his life, he believed those commands were for someone else who was somewhere else.

Then Jason, aged thirty-five and single, heard one more talk. Suddenly it hit him. If God is passionate about something, he wanted in. He wrote to me: 'I had to be a part of this. I had to be a part of God's grand cosmic restoration process that involves his care for the orphan. God's work adopting me is the life-giving, motivating, affection-stirring truth that captures my heart to engage and be involved in the care of the orphan.'[5]

God has given us a clear motivation: he has adopted us. God has given us a clear mandate: look after orphans and widows in their distress. Whatever we do to care for needy people, whether it is fighting for their rights as a lawyer, standing up for them as a politician, opening opportunities for them as a business woman, talking with them on the streets as a neighbour, opening our homes to them as a carer, or advocating for adoption like Jason does, we offer worship to God. Not just any old worship but 'pure and faultless' worship to God our Father.

Caring for vulnerable children through fostering and adoption may be a ministry that is not yet fully recognised by those in our churches, but to God it is a ministry that is flawless. It goes beyond words, rituals and pretence. It is pure and acceptable to God.

No more excuses. Something must be done, and we are the ones mandated to do the job. It is time to consider seriously the children caught up in crises through no fault of their own, and work through how we can respond and who we can help.

FOR FURTHER CONSIDERATION

Here are ten reasons you may be considering for becoming a foster carer, adoptive parent or an advocate for vulnerable children. How would you rate these in order of importance? How do each of these apply to you?

1. Because of my gut reaction.
2. Because I know the biblical mandate.
3. Because I want to become more godly.
4. Because I want to live out my faith.
5. Because I want to respond to the need.
6. Because I have time and space availability in my home and lifestyle.
7. Because I sense a calling into this ministry.
8. Because others in my household think I should.
9. Because I have experience in this area, and I have seen others involved.
10. Because I want to grow my family.

If you are unable to foster or adopt yourself, how could you help others assess their motivations for involvement, and how could you promote the best motivations within your church community?

SAM'S STORY

Between the ages of two and six I flitted in and out of different homes. I remember one specifically was filled with teenage boys, and they bullied my two younger brothers and me. It was not a positive experience.

When I was five, along with my mum, her current partner and my four brothers, I lived for a while in the downstairs of a house in Kent, with social workers living upstairs. One day I came home from a normal day at school . . . and my mum and two youngest brothers were gone. They were taken away, and I was moved into another foster home, split up from all my brothers. I didn't receive any warning or get a chance to say goodbye. To this day, I still haven't seen my two youngest brothers again.

Up to this point in my life, I had suffered abuse and severe neglect, so naturally I had a lot of problems. I was moved to a new foster family where I was able to stay for nearly three years. There I lived with two teenagers and a little girl who came to stay most weekends. I remember really struggling at school and not having many friends. However, this family looked after me very well. They valued me, treated me as an individual, and gave me many positive memories – just what I needed.

Aged eight, I moved in with a family who planned to adopt me. However, I really struggled to fit in and felt very unloved and lonely. The mother could not conceive, which is why they wanted to adopt, but ironically, while I was with them, she fell pregnant. I woke up one morning and the family were all packed to go on holiday, apart from me. Again, no warning! A social worker whom I had never seen before came and collected me and some of my belongings. I had to leave most behind.

I felt lost, lonely and completely unloved.

I then fell into the hands of a lovely Christian couple who were very welcoming and loving, and who took me to church with them. This was to have an absolutely massive impact on my life. Because of my issues and being a 'care kid' I had no friends, but at church the children seemed more compassionate and even liked me. After a while I became a strong and determined follower of Jesus. At church I also met a family who wanted to adopt me. I would ask myself, would this one really work?

Did they really love me? When would be the day they changed their mind? But they never did. They truly loved me.

CHAPTER 2

WHY KIDS END UP IN CARE AND WHERE KIDS IN CARE END UP

It was the hottest week of the year. It was so hot that when the phone rang, I even hoped it would be a cold caller. Besides, I would have been an easy sell for air-conditioning units, solar panels or a broadband package that extended to the end of the garden.

This was no cold call. It was our social service duty team hotline with the news that would change our lives forever and turn our family upside down.

After months of training, seemingly endless forms, a gruelling selection process and an inquisitorial panel interview, not to mention the extra vacuuming of the house and countless cups of coffee in a bid to impress the assessing social worker, this was the call we had been preparing for. There was a baby, a day old, who needed a foster home.

She was currently in hospital and her mother was unable to care for her. We were not told whether she would be with us for days or months or years. We were not told her racial heritage, her medical needs or her family circumstances.

We were not told what impact she would have on our lives. We could not imagine the heartstrings she would pull and the heartache she would bring.

We were just told that a baby needed caring for and could we take her in?

How could we resist?

It seemed nobody could. News travelled fast. One friend donated a Moses basket and a sackful of clothes. A neighbour sewed a beautiful handmade quilt with an underwater theme. Relatives pitched up with cameras and cards. Our church friends visited with muffins and mobiles to cuddle and coo and awkwardly congratulate.

Who could resist a small helpless baby left on a doorstep? So began *our* story of fostering and adoption.

Her story began much earlier. Maybe several generations earlier.

A large proportion of children who end up in care are the result of a persistent cycle of seriously inadequate or uninformed parenting that can leave generations of victims in its wake.

The top reasons children end up being removed from their parents are as a result of concerns that they are being physically abused, emotionally abused, sexually abused, or neglected, or as a result of family dysfunction, all of which are well-documented, recurring, cross-generational patterns.

Many people think that children go into care because they are unloved, but this assumption is misguided.

Parents generally show 'love' to their children the way they experienced being 'loved' by their parents. According to the respected psychotherapist Sue Gerhardt, if that had involved violence and chaos and neglect, then from a very young age they are wired to repeat that behaviour when they have a child of their own.[1]

There are ways of relearning these crucial skills, and as Christians on the receiving end of perfect love, we believe that people can change and should be given every chance. But in our experience of foster care, more often than we would have liked we have had to watch the cycle sadly repeat itself.

The other reason children end up in care is due to abandonment. This may be because a parent has died, or is ill, or is unable to care for the child. Sometimes it is because a child has been trafficked, or has been sent or brought to the UK without their parents. Sometimes a child is relinquished, whether at birth or occasionally later in their childhood.

Again it is easy to assume the worst of the parents. Our inbuilt sense of protection towards children makes us want to ask: who could abandon their own flesh and blood? We feel outrage. But more often than not, behind every desperate story of abandonment is a very desperate parent.

When the Bible first mentions fostering and adoption it is in the context of a desperate mother with no other option to save her family but to abandon her child. She did so in the hope that someone else would be unable to resist the small helpless baby and raise him on her behalf.

Through the bravery of five heroic women – a mother, a sister, two midwives and a princess – baby Moses escapes Pharaoh's plan to exterminate a generation of Jewish boys. It is no accident that the book of Exodus starts with a rescue. Moses was the one that got away, and the one that would, by the end of the book, rescue all of God's people from the oppression of Egyptian slavery.

Before Moses' mother relinquished her son, she had concealed him for three months. The midwives had already broken the law by not killing him during his delivery. Their civil disobedience is credited as divine obedience. But every time her baby cried, I can imagine Moses' mother feared for the lives of her whole family. As he got older and louder, she faced Sophie's choice. That impossible decision: to lose my baby or save my family?

Surrendering baby Moses in his basket to the cool of the reeds in the shallows of the river was, according to commentator Alan Cole, 'the ancient equivalent of leaving [him] on the steps of a hospital or an orphanage'.[2]

This is the original Moses basket. Actually it may be the second one. The other time this word for basket (*teba*) is used in Scripture is to describe Noah's Ark.[3] God placed eight of his children in a basket and then rescued them from a watery grave and the consequences of living without him.

When baby Moses was rescued from his watery grave, ironically it was a cry that earlier would have got his birth family executed that softened the heart of Pharaoh's daughter. It was the cry that set the course for her to become his adoptive mum.

Quick-thinking, Miriam, the sister who was watching the basket float downstream, had to brush her tears away as she plucked up the courage to offer her own family as a foster family until Moses was weaned.

So here is the first abandoned baby, the first child in foster care and the first adopted child. This could have been the happy ending to the story. But the Bible is always realistic about the complications and difficulties of family life and so we are given the whole roller-coaster story of what happens next.

Moses was rescued, and he was loved no doubt. But he also had issues. Identity issues. Confidence issues. Trust issues. These issues got him in trouble. Eventually they led to a murder, a cover-up and time on the run.

He may have been the first, but he was by no means the last castaway kid from a disrupted background who would end up on the wrong side of the law.

Twenty-seven per cent of the current prison population in the UK was once a child in care,[4] which means statistically speaking most of those convicts would have experienced abuse and neglect as a child and have offended as part of the resulting long-term legacy of emotional, developmental and behavioural disabilities. Persistent emotional damage inflicted on a child in their first few weeks and months is tragically likely to leave that child with scars for life.[5]

When an individual or a couple is assessed for adoption, the social worker has to spend a lot of time working through questions of motivation and expectation. The image of that irresistible baby sleeping sweetly in their Moses basket must also be painted alongside the sleepless nights for the new parents, and the tears that will be shed by and for that wounded child.

Moses cried aged three months old in his basket in the bulrushes. For the first time he couldn't sense that comforting presence of his mother that he had relied upon since he was conceived a year earlier. God heard his cry and arranged for a pagan princess to find him and intervene to protect and provide for him.

Many years later Moses cried again, alone in the wilderness after a human rights intervention and a murder. God heard him, and this time God himself intervened directly in that encounter by a burning bush. All those issues of confidence and trust and identity were tackled as God commissioned Moses to realise his potential and take up his vocation.

It's a powerful story. God saw Moses alone in his wilderness penitentiary just as he had seen him alone in his watery river nursery. This time God called Moses, the rescued, to become the rescuer. An ex-con, he became God's chosen leader of the Israelites, freeing them from Egyptian tyranny, poignantly rescuing them too through the river and through the wilderness.

Through the ancient story of Moses, the first ever

recorded relinquished, fostered and adopted child, God gives us a worked example of what it means to care for vulnerable children with our ears and our eyes open.

Our ears must be open to the cry of those in distress. Even a pagan princess could not ignore a helpless cry. Moses' ethnicity did not deter her. Her father's hatred of the Israelites did not deter her. The fact she had to wait for him to be weaned did not deter her. If even the daughter of the enemy can show this kind of commitment and compassion, then no less is expected of God's people.

Our eyes must be open to the possibilities and potential in each child made in God's image, however damaged they seem to be. Nobody could have guessed that rescued baby Moses would have been the one who would rescue God's people from slavery, see God with his own eyes, and lead God's people through the wilderness. God has a habit of choosing the most unlikely people to do the most amazing things and bring the greatest blessing.

Our eyes must also be open to the difficulties that may lie ahead. Moses achieved great things in his life, but it was not without long periods of turmoil. The euphoria of adding to a family through adoption will quickly be replaced by the daily challenges and rewards of parenting a child with additional struggles as a result of their displacement.

Our ears must also be open to what God is saying to us. It was through Moses that God dictated the following challenging words to be read to his rescued people throughout history as part of the blueprint of life under God's rule:

> Never take advantage of any widow or orphan. If you
> do and they cry out to me, you can be sure that I will
> hear their cry. (Exodus 22:22–23, *God's Word Translation*)

Had Pharaoh's spies heard Moses cry they would have had him killed. But it was God who heard Moses' cry and rescued him. God heard the cry of the Israelites oppressed under Egyptian slave-drivers. And through Moses, he rescued them. God hears the cry of the orphans today. And again through Moses, he warns us not to ignore them or take advantage of them.

Charlie is two. He cries with frustration. He wants to explain how he feels but he has no words. The early speech building blocks are missing from lack of inter-action as a baby.

Jack is four. He cries in the night. He can't explain why. He cannot recall the neglect and fear during the first two years of his life. But it still gives him nightmares.

Maya is ten. She cries before school. She says she hates school, but really it is the bullying. People say she is worth-less, and after ten years of hearing this message she believes it.

KC is fourteen. She cries silently. She cries out for atten-tion with a razor blade. The scars on her wrists echo her cries forever.

Najmal is seventeen. He can't cry. As an infant nobody responded to his calls for food and comfort so he stopped crying out loud. About to age out of the system, he does not have a family to go to next Christmas. There will be no proud parents at his graduation, or his wedding.

One day these children may wonder if God has heard their cry. They might ask where God was when they were being abused, or neglected, or pushed away, or left in care because they were 'unadoptable'.

We know that God has not turned a blind eye or a deaf ear to them. And the way we show it is to open our eyes and our ears, both to hear and to heed their cries.

FOR FURTHER CONSIDERATION

Here are ten groups of children that end up needing fostering and adopting. Which of these resonate with your experience, skills and availability? Which of these groups of children would you be best placed to help? What do you think the challenges would be of each group?

1. Babies.
2. Mother and baby placements.
3. Sibling groups.
4. Children with physical disabilities.
5. Children with learning difficulties.
6. Traumatised children.
7. Children from ethnic minority groups.
8. Older children.

9.   Teenagers needing long-term foster care.
10.   Unaccompanied asylum-seeking children.

If you are unable to foster or adopt yourself, which group would you be able to best support if a family at your church decided to foster or adopt?

ANDY'S STORY

I was adopted at the age of three months. As a September baby this gave my parents the perfect Christmas present (or so I like to think). I have never known any other 'status'. My parents were always open and discussed my adoption. I had a lovely storybook, which explained how special I was because I had been 'chosen' by my parents. I even got to feel I was part of the team that 'chose' my adopted brother too when I was three years old.

I have used the word 'adopted' more in the last paragraph than I do in a normal year. It is only when I am asked about a receding hairline or family history of medical conditions that I even remember I am 'adopted'. You see, it is simple. My parents are, as far as I am concerned, 100 per cent my parents. I know nothing else. For me it is a perfectly normal state of affairs. I have no longing to find my so-called birth mother. For me I have received the most perfect love and security from those I am proud to call my parents.

I only feel a connection with them and their special love. Looking back, they worked so hard and struggled – a typical hard-working family unit who made enormous sacrifices to create a loving family unit. As a shift electrician my father worked hard and for so many hours to provide for us all.

So can adoptive parents make a difference? I would certainly like to think a loving, stable home with parents who longed to have children and gave me all the love and attention they could has made much of the character I am today. As they say, 'life is not a rehearsal', so of course I cannot know what other path or direction my life would have taken if I had ended up in care or being fostered. I know statistically my life would have been a lot tougher, and the outcomes – who knows?

But what I do know is that a loving, caring family is a large part of who I am today. Without adoption I would almost certainly have never been the same person as the alternative was surely uncertainty, disruption and instability. Adoption made a massive difference to my life chances. It is not to be taken lightly but a gift to both parent and child.

Andy Reed was MP for Loughborough from 1997 to 2010. In 2012 he received an OBE for services to the community and to sport. He is now a Director of SajeImpact and chair of the Sport and Recreation Alliance.

CHAPTER 3

WHY VULNERABLE PEOPLE ARE BEST PLACED TO HELP VULNERABLE CHILDREN

'You were one of the stolen children.' Not the words you expect to hear in your fifties over a family dinner during a hot Christmas. Jim tried desperately to work out how he had never guessed that he was one of those thousands of children forcibly removed from their aboriginal mothers mostly because they were of mixed race.

A whole generation was snatched (even when there was no evidence that they had been mistreated), 'desensitised' in institutions, and then made available for adoption. The shameful secret was brought to international attention through the heart-wrenching book and film *Rabbit-Proof Fence*,[1] which told the story of three aboriginal girls aged fourteen, ten and eight, who walked the perilous fifteen hundred miles back to their mothers following the extensive fences that criss-crossed the Australian outback.

Suddenly Jim found himself comparing his skin tone to that of his siblings, revisiting his earliest memories, questioning his adoptive parents' motives, trying to piece together the puzzle of his life that only a few days ago had seemed pretty normal and mundane and together.

Who was he? Who had birthed him? Were they looking for him? Why hadn't his parents told him? Could he recall anything from his earliest family?

It was like having the rug pulled out from under his feet. It was like an earthquake where once-solid ground now ruptured and gaped with dangerous holes. It was a discovery of injustice, loss and bereavement. It was a crisis of identity.

In her book about foundlings, award-winning war correspondent Kate Adie faces her personal crisis of identity. She tells her own story of being adopted and muses a little on why adoption was often kept a secret, or at least handled discreetly around the time she was born. She concludes: 'there was an implication that the people who had chosen you could perhaps not have their own children. This was to raise the unspeakable matter of sex.'[2] Not only was the most private life of the adopters suddenly felt to be on public display, but a foundling too was commonly assumed to be the product of an illegitimate liaison, or the child of a prostitute. Adie's conclusion was that the combined effect of the contraceptive pill, the legalising of abortion, and fewer taboos regarding sex and single motherhood have thankfully paved the way for adoption to become less of an embarrassment for most adopters and adoptees.

Nowadays, adoptive parents are counselled to tell the children from an early age that they are adopted. They are encouraged to celebrate the fact that a biological parent gave and chose life for the child, to explain the reasons they were unable to care for them, to celebrate that a foster parent loved and looked after them and that finally they were hand-picked to be the child's forever family and offered a home for good. In many homes, Adoption Day is celebrated like a second birthday.

This does not inoculate adopted children from a later crisis of identity, or prevent the questions or the feelings of injustice, loss and bereavement. But it no longer hits like an earthquake, shattering their emotional security, robbing them in an instant of every foundation and familiarity.

One tangible way a child is helped to understand their past and their identity is by means of a life-story book given to each adoptee. The personalised life-story book explains to a child their history and the homes they have been in. It describes birth families, foster families and adopting families – the good bits and the bad bits.

Words and pictures explain some significant times in the child's life. When they first went to school. When they had to go to hospital. When they had to change foster carer. When they had to appear in court. When they achieved a milestone. Where they spent their birthdays. Why the professionals made the decisions they did.

A life-story book is a precious keepsake. It recognises that a child's past – their heritage and experiences and memories – cannot simply be erased, but needs to be acknowledged, worked through, understood, even treasured.

It cannot cover every detail, and so there will always be gaps, but it goes some way to answering the main questions – Who? What? Why? When? Where?

Children who are adopted typically begin to ask these questions around the age of six, and by the time they are teenagers they can become quite obsessed with them, along with other anxieties that rear their heads as they metamorphose from a child into an adult. Often, but not always, even as adults, they may be haunted by the holes or the hurts in their early memories and histories.

The life-story book is sometimes all a child has to go on to find answers and, by referring to it often in a safe and supportive environment, it is hoped that the child can learn to live with and even love their own story. Eventually, as an adult, they will be able to supplement it by requesting access to more information from their files, if they so wish.

I often think it would be good if everybody had a life-story book. Most of us have access to a parent or sibling or other relative when we have questions about our origins or our early years. Gradually we build up a mental timeline that helps us reflect on who we are. Nevertheless, we all come from flawed families, to a greater or lesser degree, and bear scars and insecurities from our childhood experiences. Sadly we are not always encouraged to reflect on these, and many of us often brush them under the carpet.

Hiding those wounds and vulnerabilities away can be a recipe for disaster. Sometimes it can cause us to put up barriers and facades that prevent us relating at a deep level with others,[3] those who may be struggling with the same problems, but who are also trying to disguise the fact.

Our insecurities often surface in the context of our marriages and parenting, potentially hurting those we love the most. It is also a common experience of foster carers and adopters. As we often see in families in crisis, unaddressed trauma doesn't seem to go away – it comes back again and again.

If we want to start helping vulnerable children come to terms with traumas and tragedies in their past, we may need to start by recognising our own vulnerabilities.

This should dispel the myth that only 'super-parents' can adopt and foster. The fact that we struggle as people, as parents and as believers does not eliminate us from the task of fostering and adoption. On the contrary, the best people to understand the vulnerable are those who know they too are vulnerable.

This should also enable us to understand better the process kids in care need to go through as they try to reconcile their past and future and cope with the emotional impact it has on their day-to-day behaviour and outlook on life.

This should also prepare us for when those scars open unexpectedly. Our underlying issues can often be triggered when caring for traumatised children, and we need to be ready, equipped to recognise what is happening and seek appropriate help.

Also, recognising that we and most people around us are living with scars from our childhood will help us become a community where these things are more openly discussed, and where we find support from each other. Church-run parenting courses are one place where this is starting to happen naturally, and perhaps more children will be prevented from ending up in care because the church is facilitating this vital ministry.

Finally, admitting that we are broken breaks down the 'us and them' barriers when we are trying to help broken children. The Indian missionary D. T. Niles described Christian mission as 'one beggar telling another beggar where to find bread'. We are not superior to the children in care we are trying to support, or the often broken families they have been removed from. Remembering we are all wounded and needy will help us find non-patronising, non-threatening, non-condescending ways to get alongside and support children in need and their families.

This equalising and equipping through shared experience is what God seems to be saying to his people in the book of Deuteronomy: you once suffered at the hands of oppressors – now you are freed to help others who are suffering in the same way. In the extract below, this link is stressed twice by means of a command, once at the beginning and once at the end:

> Do not deprive the foreigner or the fatherless of justice, or take the cloak of the widow as a pledge. Remember

that you were slaves in Egypt and the Lord your God redeemed you from there. That is why I command you to do this.

When you are harvesting in your field and you overlook a sheaf, do not go back to get it. Leave it for the foreigner, the fatherless and the widow, so that the Lord your God may bless you in all the work of your hands. When you beat the olives from your trees, do not go over the branches a second time. Leave what remains for the foreigner, the fatherless and the widow. When you harvest the grapes in your vineyard, do not go over the vines again. Leave what remains for the foreigner, the fatherless and the widow. Remember that you were slaves in Egypt. That is why I command you to do this. (Deuteronomy 24:17–22)

God knows that if we can brush our own problems under the carpet, we sadly are cruelly capable of brushing other people's problems under the carpet too.

Twice he commands the Israelites to recall their suffering, and then in response to reach out to the 'foreigner, fatherless and widow' suffering around them. They were to rescue them from their otherwise invisible, inconsequential status, just as they had been rescued themselves.

The book of Deuteronomy is a useful book to read if you are considering fostering or adopting.

First, because, together with the rest of the Bible, it is our life-story book. It helps set our lives in the context of all that God has been doing with our spiritual ancestors, and helps us affirm our own identity and vocation.

Second, because it was written to God's people at a time of huge transition, as they had left behind their temporary homes in the desert and moved into their forever home in the Promised Land. At this point, between the horrors of their history and the hope of a happily-ever-after ending, God knew that his people needed a reality check to keep perspective on both the life they were leaving behind and the security they were about to enjoy.

The passage above challenges us not to forget our own experience of tough times, but to sear it into our memories for the sake of other people around us. Then, between the two commands to 'Remember', God gives some instructions as to how practically we could help the vulnerable around us. There are three key principles here that are directly applicable to us and how we relate to children in care.

The first is that we are told to take responsibility for the vulnerable. These verses were not written for kings or governments or the Department of Work and Pensions, but for farmers. Ordinary working people are to play their part in providing for children in care.

God wouldn't have needed to stress this if it was obvious or easy. It was counter-intuitive and counter-cultural then, as it is now. Caring for the poor remains a significant way the Church can show that we have alternative values to those of the world.

The second principle is to offer dignity to the vulnerable.

The farmers were not instructed to collect all the harvest and then just drop off a token basket of goodies at the local orphanage. They were told to be careful to be careless in their gathering of crops, deliberately leaving plenty behind for others to glean.

This practice is illustrated in the beautiful story of widow refugee Ruth, struggling to make ends meet as she cared for her widowed elderly mother-in-law. She was on the receiving end of the generosity of landowner Boaz, who ended up falling in love with Ruth and becoming the provider for both women.

God wanted his people with enough to go round to say 'Help yourselves' to those who had nothing. This is not charity. This is a generous empowering of the vulnerable. This is sensitivity to the dignity of others that must be displayed as we work with children in care and their often-impoverished families.

The last principle is to enjoy proximity with the vulnerable. There is an assumption here of intermingling. The poor were not restricted to the edges of the cities, or ghettoised, or managed in camps where food aid was airlifted in. People from different life situations and cultures were welcomed onto the property and into the community.

Soup runs and food banks are fantastic initiatives. Thank God for all those who donate time and effort and supplies. But if we want to step it up, we can learn some radical hospitality from Deuteronomy.

Give the vulnerable access, make them welcome, provide

for them, empower them. Be soft-hearted and even-handed towards them. Invite them into your houses saying, 'Make yourselves at home, and help yourselves to what you need.'

This is the invitation Rachel and Jason decided to issue. For them, adoption in the wake of their own personal struggles and in light of God's mercy throughout history was a 'no-brainer'. Here is their story.

> When we discovered that we were infertile it became difficult for us not to have a rosy image of what being a parent must be like. Even when our friend's kids were running through the house screaming blue murder, something in our hearts said, 'If only they were our kids, running through our house screaming blue murder!' Facing the fact that the noisy and beautiful family we had imagined for ourselves might not happen was hard. But it wasn't the end for us.
>
> Our journey so far with adoption hasn't been without heartache. There have been losses and we've needed to grieve. We've appreciated all the prayers of friends who have longed with us for our own biological children. We've had prophecies that we will have our own bio-logical children and prophecies that we won't! But we're not sure if we would change anything about our path to parenthood. Becoming adoptive parents has given us a deeper awareness of the privilege and challenges of good parenting and we've woken up to the fact that whether

we raise biological, step, fostered or adopted children, none of us parent alone. God parents alongside us.

This fills us with such confidence as we build our family, adopted child by adopted child. We know the grief of being childless and we have experienced God's power and presence in our pain. But deeper than this lies God's yearning desire for every child to be in a loving family.

Does God really want us to be parents? For us it's a no-brainer. Not because we've had a flash of spiritual insight or because we think that adoption is a 'noble cause', but because there's something deeply instinctual and practical about God's desire to put the vulnerable and broken in families. He's done it with us, we want to do it for our children.[4]

FOR FURTHER CONSIDERATION

Here are ten questions to help you think through the impact fostering or adopting may have on you personally. Highlight those areas where you will need specific support, professional help or personal training.

1. How could fostering/adopting impact your marriage or marriage prospects?
2. How could fostering/adopting impact the way you relate to any birth children?

3. How would you cope with children displaying challenging behaviour?
4. How would you cope with working together with social workers or professionals?
5. How would you help a child process their grief and loss?
6. To what extent could you rely on wider family and church family to provide support?
7. How would you cope with relating to birth families and facilitating contact and reunification or reconciliation where appropriate?
8. What traumas from your past may be triggered by helping traumatised children?
9. How do you cope with stress, anxiety and disappointment?
10. Who would you share the incredible joys and rewards of fostering and adopting with?

If you are unable to foster or adopt yourself, how could you inform yourself about these issues to help others going through the process?

DIANE'S STORY

When my sister, a single mum of three, decided to go back to college, I shared some of the childcare with her, which included having Justine, her youngest, staying with me on a regular basis.

A year later my sister suddenly died. It was immediately and unanimously agreed that my sister's children would remain within our family. Justine, then aged two, chose to live with me. I became her mum literally overnight!

Justine was a particular blessing to me in those early days as we went through a time of bereavement together. She demonstrated the astonishing healing a person can bring to you in the midst of you caring for them.

Justine is now happily married with children of her own. But it doesn't stop my concern for her. In fact, I'm assured this is the normal way of life. Children need parents who can love them intentionally and unconditionally for their entire lives. This, I believe, is the bedrock of society.

Last year when I lost my parents, I felt abandoned, even after five decades of having them around. So I can only imagine how tough it is for children who lose their parents after just a few months or years. I think it's important for us all to consider what we can do to help hurting children find a family for the long run.

I believe parenting is one of the hardest, most heartbreaking jobs anyone can do. It's also the most incredible, satisfying, rewarding gift any of us can ever receive. I highly recommend it. Family is the greatest blessing.

Diane Louise Jordan is a television and radio presenter, inspirational speaker and author.

CHAPTER 4

WHY CHILDREN NEED HOMES, NOT CHILDREN'S HOMES

Water was dripping from the polystyrene ceiling into plastic buckets carefully positioned along the bare corridor. Beige paint was blistering from the walls and we felt like we were wading through the damp air. A serious DIY disaster zone, surely this institution was no place for a baby. Definitely this was no place for my foster baby.

We had cared for her since birth and now nine months later she was moving into this mother and baby placement unit. Leaving our precious bundle in such decrepit conditions by order of the court was difficult for us, to put it mildly.

But we were powerless to argue.

Another baby. This time in the pristine and sterile state-of-the-art local children's hospital. Fighting for every breath in the intensive care unit with tubes and monitors and a strict routine of medication, my wife would sit next to her night after night, for month after month, unable to hold back the tears.

We felt powerless.

On these occasions I turned to the Bible to be reminded of the one who holds all things in his hands.

> May God arise, may his enemies be scattered;
>   may his foes flee before him.
> May you blow them away like smoke –
>   as wax melts before the fire,
>   may the wicked perish before God.
> But may the righteous be glad
>   and rejoice before God;
>   may they be happy and joyful.
>
> Sing to God, sing praise to his name,
>   extol him who rides on the clouds;
>   rejoice before him – his name is the Lord.
> A father to the fatherless, a defender of widows,
>   is God in his holy dwelling.
> God sets the lonely in families,
>   he leads out the prisoners with singing;
>   but the rebellious live in a sun-scorched land.
> (Psalm 68:1–6)

I love this psalm. The first line is a direct quote from Numbers. The part where the Ark of the Covenant is publicly led out to a chorus of 'May God arise'.[1] And the whole psalm would have been sung as David processed with the Ark up to Jerusalem.

For a boy who grew up wanting to be Indiana Jones, defeating the bad guys, smashing his way out of trouble, rescuing the victims and discovering the Ark of the Covenant for myself, this psalm is a powerful antidote to feelings of powerlessness.

Another ark!

Not the huge wooden one that Noah built or the mini woven one that protected Moses. This heavy, insect-resistant, acacia-wood, gilded ark contained the two rocks inscribed with God's Ten Commandments. It was a national treasure, symbolising the special relationship they had with God. And when the people of Israel went into battle, the Ark of the Covenant went ahead as a sign that God was with them. Joshua used it when he and his army famously conquered the city-citadel of Jericho.

In the context of celebrating and processing with this gold box about the size of a child's cot, this psalm portrays God as the one who won't fit in the box, because he rides the clouds. God is so powerful that even his strongest enemies appear as solid as smoke and as resilient as wax.[2]

And what does this mighty God wield his power for? He uses his cloud-riding authority and enemy-melting justice to come to the aid of the weak and defenceless. His power is put at the disposal of the powerless. He jumps to the rescue of widows and orphans.

The Lord introduces himself as father to the fatherless, defender of widows.

This is a striking juxtaposition of the description of an uncontainable all-powerful enemy-melting God with his tenderness and care for vulnerable children.

And in this context comes what may be the most shocking verse of all: 'God sets the lonely in families.'

However insignificant and inadequate we feel before his terrifying invincibility, God still entrusts us with his precious children.

I often feel inadequate as a parent, even by much lower standards. I can't say that I have never lost any of my children in TK Maxx. I can't tell you I have never forgotten to pick my children up from football training. I can't tell you that I didn't pass on any of my annoying breakfast cereal eating habits. I can't tell you that I didn't accidentally scar my son for life while walking my neighbour's dog on its temperamental retractable lead. I can't tell you that I didn't once find a plastic toy in my toddler's toy-box that was actually a phone-shaped working cigarette lighter. I can't tell you that my kids are perfectly balanced, perfectly behaved, perfectly turned-out angels. They are not, and neither am I. If you ask them, they will probably fistfight over who gets to catalogue my shortcomings as a father.

Nevertheless, by God's grace, in his wisdom and by his decree, he takes our flawed families and homes and commandeers them for the good of the defenceless.

Arianne grew up in a turbulent home. Her father was an abusive alcoholic. Her mother had a severe mental health issue that caused frequent hospitalisations. They divorced when she was seven after the suicide of her eldest brother. Arianne spent periods in various foster homes, eighteen months in a church-run women's refuge and periods of being back home where she was the primary carer for her younger siblings.

When Arianne was fifteen, her mother attempted suicide again, and social services finally intervened to place all the children in care. The only family who came forward for Arianne were some Christians who had got to know her a little while she was at their church's women's refuge. They already had two children, including an adopted daughter with additional needs, but nevertheless they offered to take in both Arianne and her youngest sister.

Initially it was tough going for everyone and it took a long time for Arianne to adapt. But this is what she writes in hindsight:

> My foster family in lifestyle, happiness, choices, beliefs could not have been more different than what I knew. It took a long time to stop mothering my little sister, and to start looking after myself. I had a terrible self-image, deep-set apathy and almost hatred for life, as I had experienced little or no joy, but my foster family showered me with grace, love, and affirmation. It took a long time to stop swearing, acting in a self-destructive way, and to accept their ways of living, and that we could be a family. Until this day, I am so utterly thankful to God for their self-sacrifice and willingness to do this.

Arianne has become a strong advocate for this biblical principle of seeing the lonely set in families. She knows from her own experience with bad foster carers that this calling is not for everybody. But she insists that the Church should be leading the way in welcoming children into our homes: 'I believe anyone in church if capable, whether they have their own children or not, should make room in their lives for those children who need homes. I believe that it is a biblical principle, and one of the best ways possible, to show in a practical, everyday way the love of God, and to literally be able to transform someone's life.'

Going into care at the age of fifteen, statistically Arianne should have been taken in not by a family but by a children's home. Around one in ten children in care live in a residential children's home, usually those who are in their late teens or who are struggling with significant behavioural issues. For some children, a good children's home, with committed, trained staff and a family atmosphere, can offer significant advantages over a foster home. There is less pressure to 'fit in', better understanding of the child's difficulties, and a stronger chance of siblings being able to stay together.

Children in their late teens are less likely to be placed in foster homes, and tragically they are also considered 'unadoptable'. It seems that hardly anyone comes forward to offer a home to children in this age bracket.

With the combination of experience of family breakdown and adolescent emotional turmoil, it is true that no adoptive family would be in for an easy ride. The unspoken understanding is that social workers believe it would not be worth it for a family to invest in these children, as they will soon be old enough to fend for themselves. Statistically it is these children who age out of the system without families who are most at risk of unemployment, homelessness and imprisonment.

Perhaps we need to challenge the assumption that nobody would come forward to adopt a troubled teen. Without a family they will have nowhere to call home, not only for the last few years of dependency, but for the rest of their lives. Without a family they will have nowhere to go for their Christmas dinner. No one to call if they end up in hospital. No one to celebrate with them as they get a qualification or a new job. No one to text for some advice on how long to leave a casserole in the oven. No one to send a Mother's Day card to. No one to give them away at a wedding. No one to present a grandchild to.

Some teenagers are acutely aware of the ticking clock – they know that if they don't find a family in the next couple of years, all hope is lost of ever feeling like they really belong somewhere. Some teenagers would give their right arm to be adopted.

For those of us who are feeling cautious about the practicalities of taking in a young child, it may be that offering a home to a teenager is a real possibility. It may be that we could set a trend to show love and inclusion to a whole generation of children for whom homelessness and destitution are the path of least resistance. This may be the biggest contribution the Church could make today to change society, in one move relieving the foster care system, relieving the prisons, relieving the abortion clinics, relieving the mental health units, relieving the problem of homelessness. The power of being set in a family is not to be underestimated.

One night in 1867 Thomas, a young trainee doctor, was taken by a young boy called Jim on a trip around the streets of London that changed his life. The lad led Thomas to a rooftop in Whitechapel, where hundreds of boys were sleeping rough, and to a turning point in his life. The young medic had planned to serve as a cross-cultural missionary in China but instead founded an orphanage where he aimed to feed, clothe and educate the homeless and destitute children of London. When Dr Thomas Barnardo died, there were some eight and a half thousand children being cared for in ninety-six centres.

George Muller in Bristol and Amy Carmichael in India also have remarkable stories of how they impacted a whole country through faithfully obeying God's call to start orphanages. Countless other Christians have followed in their footsteps to care for vulnerable children in children's homes all over the world.

Orphanages have literally saved the lives of innumerable children. They have rescued children from workhouses, slums, streets, prisons, wars, brothels and slavery all around the world. They have provided food, shelter, company, education, hope and a sense of community in many countries.

Barnardo's no longer runs orphanages. They honour the legacy of Dr Barnardo by providing for vulnerable children through supporting fostering and adoption – not because foster and adoptive families can replace birth families, but because a family environment is proven to be the place where children are most likely to thrive.

Imagine if children you know were to be tragically orphaned. If you could choose to place them in an orphanage or to place them in a family, which would you choose for them? In the event that my wife and I are killed in a car accident, we haven't reserved a place in a local children's home. Our will makes it very clear that guardians have been appointed so they can be brought up in a family home.

Kay and Rick Warren from Saddleback church in Orange County, USA, recently stated that the vision of their church is not to open orphanages, but to close them down. Their hope is that orphans everywhere would find a family to care for them. There are charities working all round the world, particularly in countries where terrible conditions of orphanages have come to light, to shift the system to supporting local adoption and fostering as the primary means of hope for these children.

God knew this from Day One: he is the God who sets the lonely in families.

David, who wrote Psalm 68, knew what it was like to be lonely. He had come from a large family with six older brothers and two sisters. But when he was about sixteen years old, he had to leave them behind to begin his new job singing and fighting for King Saul. During his time living in the palace he became close to Saul's son Jonathan, but this relationship was to be wrenched away from him too. Intensely jealous of David, King Saul banished him. David then spent around fifteen years in exile, and many of the psalms are heartfelt cries of loneliness and distress from this period of his life. Eventually David became king, had his own family and, indeed, a dynasty.

But King David never forgot the truth that God sets the lonely in families. He had experienced it for himself; now he felt it was his turn to pass on the blessing.

Remembering his valued friendship with Jonathan, David asked around about what happened to his family after he had been killed in battle, and when he found out that there was one dependent son left, he effectively adopted him. Mephibosheth had been orphaned and crippled at the age of five, but his emotional scars and permanent physical disabilities were no obstacle to David's love. He provided for him not only financially, but treated him like a son, ensuring he always joined him at mealtimes.[3]

A mighty king using his power and influence to set the lonely in families – this was what David knew about God, what David loved about God, and what David aspired to emulate. The Bible commends David as a man after God's own heart,[4] and as a man to aspire to emulate ourselves. Through his psalms and through his home life, David inspires us to know his God, father to the fatherless, and challenges us to be like his God, who sets the lonely in families.

FOR FURTHER CONSIDERATION

Here are ten questions to help you assess how a foster or adoptive child may impact your home.

1. Are you willing to allow social workers total access to your home, family, finances, relationships in order to complete an assessment?
2. Are you willing to make the necessary changes to your house to comply with guidelines for fostering and adopting children?
3. To what extent are you expecting the children to adapt to your way of family?
4. To what extent are you prepared to shift your way of doing family to include a new member?
5. How would fostering or adopting impact family occasions, family photographs, family holidays and family traditions?
6. How would you introduce a foster/adopted child to your family?
7. How would your wider family accept and support foster/adopted children?
8. How many spare rooms do you have and how could they be set up for a child?

9. How would you handle those significant first few minutes of meeting a child?
10. Where would you turn if you needed help?

If you are not able to foster or adopt, try to think through the implications for foster and adoptive families in your church, so you can better understand and support them.

DAN'S STORY

There is no such thing as adoption without suffering, whether we are talking about a person's adoption of a child (little 'a' adoption) or of God the Father's Adoption of us (big 'A' Adoption). Suffering and adoption/Adoption always go together, and what an amazing story/Story they collaborate to write – a Story that helps grow our understanding of what a theology of Adoption is.

At the centre of my family's adoption story was the gracious work of God through Jesus' 'Abba! Father!' cry and the life and death of my firstborn son Daniel, who was born in 1999 and died three years later on 19 November 2002. Between his birth and death were three years of unrelenting suffering. Since there were only a handful of days when his body was not ravaged by between forty and seventy seizures a day, I can rarely think of him without some measure of pain. But it's through the pain of those memories that our 'Abba! Father!' continues to take me deeper into the Story of his work of Adoption within the history of redemption.

During the last few weeks of my son's life, I slept almost every night with him in his room in the intensive care unit. Those night hours increasingly became terrifying for me. On a couple of occasions, I was jerked out of sleep by nurses rushing into the room to resuscitate him. So as the evening hours of each day approached, I would feel intense stress. Wondering if he would die in the night while I slept next to him was taking a serious toll on me. I was spiritually, physically and emotionally spent.

For three years I had witnessed my son's unremitting suffering. His suffering was my suffering. Every time I helplessly watched a seizure wreak havoc on his body, pain ripped through my heart. Day after day after day, for three straight years, we watched him suffer like this.

One evening during the last week of his life, I sat down next to his bed to read Isaiah 53 in hope of finding some refuge, some relief from my inner turmoil and fear.

It was within that context that the gospel light of Isaiah 53:4, 'Surely he has borne our griefs and carried our sorrows' (ESV), and Mark 14:36, Jesus' 'Abba! Father!' cry in Gethsemane, broke into my heart. Suddenly, I saw more beauty in those two verses than I had ever seen before. Surely, I thought, Jesus has borne my griefs and carried my sorrows. When he cried 'Abba! Father!' in Gethsemane, he was crying for me in my place!

Then it hit me: Jesus bore our griefs. He bore our sorrows. He cried 'Abba! Father!' for us! It's remarkable enough that Jesus bore my sorrows, as heavy as I now feel them to be. To think that Jesus would do that for me! But he also bore the sorrows of all of his people. If the sorrows I am bearing are crushing me, imagine the weight Jesus was under when he bore all of our sorrows. Oh how Jesus has loved us!

In those moments of meditation I experienced more of the depth of Jesus' love for me than I ever had before. The words of Isaiah 53:4 became my fear-conquering experience of Galatians 4:6, 'God has sent the Spirit of his Son into our hearts, crying, "Abba! Father!"' (*ESV*)

One lesson I learned that night is that central to a theology of Adoption is Jesus' life and death for me, for us.

> *Dan Cruver is an adoptive father of two and Director of Together for Adoption, an organisation helping to equip the Church for global orphan care.*

CHAPTER 5

WHY RELIEVING SUFFERING MEANS RECEIVING SUFFERING

He seemed to be the answer to his parents' dreams. Finally a baby boy after three little girls – now the family was complete. The proud mum who had been so desperate for a son was ecstatic. She named him Peter.

Seventeen months later the London Ambulance Service received a 999 call and paramedics rushed to the scene to find that little Peter had died in his cot. He was covered in bruises. His ribs were broken. His spine had been snapped. Further investigation showed that this little toddler had been used as a human punch bag more than once.

The tragedy was made even worse by the fact that in the last eight months of his short life he had been seen on sixty separate occasions by health and social workers. This included an appointment with a consultant paediatrician two days before his death, and a concerning phone call to a social worker just twenty-four hours before he died.

The case of Baby P caused national outcry.

As the court convicted Peter's mother, her boyfriend and her lodger of causing or allowing the death of a child, the questions came thick and fast. Why didn't anyone do anything to help him? How could sixty people have missed this brutality? How come nobody intervened?

For Christians there are other questions we may ask or be asked. Did God hear him cry? Why did the father to the fatherless not intervene? Surely God was a witness to the beatings – why did he not rescue him instead of watching as the life drained out of him and he slowly turned blue?

Violence against the vulnerable. Undeserved abuse. The suffering of the innocent has troubled philosophers through history. For the Algerian philosopher Albert Camus the suffering of children was another reason not to believe in God at all.

> [F]or many months now death had shown no favour-
> itism – but they had never yet watched a child's agony
> minute by minute, as they had now been doing since
> daybreak. Needless to say, the pain inflicted on these
> innocent victims had always seemed to them to be what
> in fact it was: an abominable thing. 'My God, spare this
> child!' But the wail continued without cease.[1]

Similarly, for the character Ivan Karamazov in Dostoyevsky's masterpiece novel, the trauma faced by young children was enough for him to want to hand God back the 'ticket' to eternal life.

Pray tell me, what have children got to do with it? It's quite incomprehensible . . .[2]

How do Christians respond to the terrible suffering of children and this huge obstacle to many people's faith?

First of all we must not shy away from this issue just as the subject of suffering is not ignored in the Bible. In fact a framework of hope is offered to help us face suffering as the whole story of Scripture revolves around an innocent Son suffering on behalf of a guilty world.

The Bible teaches categorically that God is perfect, loving, just and all-knowing and that he created the world – a place that was ideal for human flourishing.

The Bible teaches that we the human race chose to turn our back on him. This choice has produced a chain reaction of broken relationships that affect everything about us and our world.

The Bible teaches that God himself relinquished his own Son: to grow up with the slur of dubious parentage; to become a toddler refugee in Egypt; to be labelled a trouble-maker in the eyes of synagogue and state; to become an innocent victim of inhuman cruelty; to be used as a punch bag, beaten, bruised, brutally executed and buried.

The Bible teaches that God raised Jesus up from the dead, vindicating him of all guilt, returning him to his position in heaven with his Father.

The Bible teaches that this death on the cross was not just some miscarriage of justice, political stunt or accident of history. But that through Jesus' sacrifice God is putting all things right, restoring peace to the world and starting a revolution of healing that will leave no person or place untouched.

Jesus' followers started a quiet revolution, which began in a small backwater of the Roman Empire two thousand years ago and then spread like yeast in dough throughout geography and history. It has led Christians throughout the centuries to provide for widows and orphans, care for plague-infected neighbours, fight slavery and child labour, oppose apartheid in South Africa, campaign for racial equality in America, and outlaw wife-burning in India. It has led to you picking up this book and considering your role in the lives of vulnerable children. It has led to us working together to see if we can give the world a taste of things to come by sharing God's mercy and compassion here and now.

The Bible teaches that one day this revolution will lead to a restoration where God's kingdom comes on earth as it is in heaven, and encourages us to play our part in that restoration right now.

But the Bible gives no explanation of why sometimes God miraculously intervenes, and why sometimes he allows families to go through terrible tragedies.

The Bible gives no promises that Christians will be immune from suffering.

The Bible gives no formulae for working out when suffering is deserved and when it isn't.

The Bible gives no neat solutions, no quick-fix prayers or ready-to-use guidelines for what to do when you or your loved ones suffer.

When the Bible tackles the question of suffering head on, it does so by devoting an entire book, forty-two chapters, to the topic. That's more chapters than any of the Gospels.

When the Bible debates the problem of suffering, it does not focus on impersonal statistics, but hones in on one man in the middle of extreme suffering.

The epic tale of Job asks more questions than it offers solutions. Perhaps it is God's way of saying that it is OK to probe and protest and pray about the injustices and calamities in our world.

Job's story is truly heartbreaking. He loses his business. He loses his possessions. His employees are killed in a fire. He loses his children, all ten of them. He loses his health. His friends lose faith in him and he almost loses his faith. It is a book of multiple tragedies.

Troubles crowd in on Job on all fronts simultaneously.

Perhaps you have experienced this in your own life.

When a child comes into care he or she, like Job, has most likely suffered not just one tragedy, but multiple tragedies.

First the child may lose their sense of security, as a parent derails. Then they may lose their health, as their care becomes inconsistent. Their confidence plummets. Then a crisis occurs and they are taken into care. At that moment they lose everything else: their family, their friends, their belongings, their school. They lose their connections, their power, their dignity, their identity.

As a foster carer and as a pastor I have heard the most horrendous stories of family breakdown and have seen at first hand the impact such breakdown has on the lives of children that I come to love.

I have seen close up how drug addiction so warps the minds of fathers that they choose to feed their habits rather than feed their children.

I have met mothers who prostitute their own daughters to other family members.

I have seen the cyclical pattern of abuse – where the abused become the abusers.

I have seen children who after being removed from physical torture, then spend years dealing with the aftermath in mental torture.

I have asked social workers a lot of questions. Is this birth parent getting enough support? Is this child going to turn out okay? Are you sure the adoptive family will love this child? Why hasn't that suffering sibling been removed yet? What if the violent uncle finds out where I live? Who will help this child give evidence against her family member? Why is there such a long wait for treatment?

When answers are in short supply or a long time in coming, then I redirect my questions to God.

There is no doubt that getting involved with vulnerable children forces you to have a prayer life.

There are times when you will burst with praise for the

opportunity of joining in with what God is doing in helping and healing tiny broken hearts.

There are also times when your heart will be breaking because of the broken lives you come across. Not just the children you are caring for, but a whole blast zone of fractured relationships.

There are times when you just fall before God with the one big question: why do bad things happen to good people?

This is the whole premise of the book of Job.

The book starts with a behind-the-scenes view of what is going on in Job's life. There is a conversation that takes place in heaven, between Satan the Accuser and God the Almighty.

Do human beings only love God because he is good to them? Do humans just love the good things they get from God and not God himself?

It's a fair question. It comes up in every relationship. For example – do my children love me as their father, or do they love me as their bank clerk, taxi driver, personal shopper, live-in chef and hotel manager? Is it a consumptive relationship on their part? Do they calculate in their heads, 'What can affection get me today?' Or is it a transactional relationship on my part? Do I tot up in my mind, 'What kind of present will buy their affection?'

If everything were stripped away, would my kids still love me? If everything were stripped away, would you still love God? Job's life is a test case for humanity.

To answer Satan's question, God allows a blameless, righteous person to suffer to demonstrate that it is possible to love God as a heavenly Father, not a divine sugar daddy. Through Job, God proves that humanity can love God in spite of suffering rather than because of blessing.

Job, our test subject, is a paragon of virtue and his holiness is not restricted to avoiding evil and pious religious attendance. Job is not a foster carer or an adoptive parent but his commitment to vulnerable children has shaped his home life, his work life and his spiritual life.

> If I have denied the desires of the poor
>   or let the eyes of the widow grow weary,
> if I have kept my bread to myself,
>   not sharing it with the fatherless –
> but from my youth I reared them as a father would,
>   and from my birth I guided the widow –
> if I have seen anyone perishing for lack of clothing,
>   or the needy without garments,
> and their hearts did not bless me
>   for warming them with the fleece from my sheep,
> if I have raised my hand against the fatherless,
>   knowing that I had influence in court,
> then let my arm fall from the shoulder,
>   let it be broken off at the joint.
> For I dreaded destruction from God,
>   and for fear of his splendour I could not do such
>   things.
> (Job 31:16–23)

Not many of us would be able to measure up to Job's level of active, radical obedience to God.

Job has served the poor, shared food with orphans, cared for vulnerable children since he was a child, clothed the naked, and used his influence and power for the benefit of the fatherless.

Despite all of this service and unparalleled compassionate care, Job still suffers.

Those involved in protecting vulnerable children do not get special privileges from God. They are not an elite class of Christian with a 'get-out-of-suffering-free' card.

One of America's most well-known Christian songwriters and worship leaders bears testimony to this. Steven Curtis Chapman with his wife Mary Beth had three birth children and adopted three more from China. Together they set up a charity that has helped provide homes for over two thousand waiting children, and started a medical care centre in China that provides holistic care to orphans with special needs. Yet all this ministry did not protect them from suffering. On 21 May 2008 their adopted daughter ran out to meet her older brother. As he swung the car into the driveway he did not see five-year-old Maria Sue until it was fatally too late. Mary Beth tells the heart-wrenching story in her book *Choosing to See*.[3] She writes:

> The chronic pain that lives in my heart and my soul wants surgery to fix it . . . get it better quick! But sixteen months into this journey, I'm beginning to realize that

God perhaps wants me to heal slowly so that as many things that can be learned about him are learned . . . I am trusting He has the Chapmans' best plan scripted out for us until we are with sweet Maria again. I'm sure it won't be all happy and pain free. I know that suffering is one place where He ministers to us the most. So to think we've had our quota would be foolish. I am just longing for the day when all the pain stops.[4]

Choosing to relieve suffering for others does not inoculate us from suffering ourselves. In fact by involving ourselves in the pain of others, we effectively invite pain and trouble in. There is something beautiful and Christlike about choosing a path of suffering alongside others for their sake.

Kevin and Cindy's first foster placement was a three-month-old baby girl with complex medical needs. The first night baby Katie was in their home she stopped breathing. Fortunately Kevin knew how to perform CPR and resuscitated her, but it was one of many scares as they cared for this extremely ill little girl over the following months. Meanwhile the social workers had been unable to reunite her with her family and were looking for an adoptive family for Katie. They did not have to look far. Jayne Schooler was one of the social workers involved who fought on Kevin and Cindy's behalf for them to adopt their foster daughter. She wrote the following to the sceptical attorney who couldn't understand and therefore questioned Kevin and Cindy's motives:

Kevin and Cindy live by a higher principle in life. It is called VRS:

V stands for Voluntary. No one is forcing them to make this lifelong commitment to Katie. They are doing it out of supreme love for her. R stands for Redemptive. Redemption means to restore dignity to a person whose life situations are difficult, painful and heartbreaking. Such were Katie's. S stands for Suffering. Suffering means the loss of something for the sake of another. Kevin and Cindy have paid a high cost. Emotionally, physically, financially – in every way they have suffered. They would not call it that, but that is exactly what it is. This is why Kevin and Cindy are adopting Katie.[5]

Although Jesus teaches us that as Christians we are to take up our cross daily, we still struggle with the problem of suffering. Like Job's well-intentioned friends whose so-called comfort makes up the majority of the book, we often have a very confused understanding. Although included in God's inspired and infallible word, their advice is actually insensitive drivel and fallacious, if pious, theology. God's scathing verdict on them is 'I am angry with you' (Job 42:7). They think they are helping, but they are making things worse.

When Geoff and Jennifer adopted a child with severe learning difficulties, many people in the church prayed for the struggling family and for the child. But instead of signs of improvement, the difficulties continued unabated. After a while somebody from the church challenged the couple:

'Do you think there is an unconfessed sin in your life or the child's life?'

The friend may have been well-meaning, but Geoff and Jennifer were devastated. The one place they thought they would find solace and sanctuary was their church community, but instead they felt that they were being accused and treated as somehow guilty for their child's suffering.

The book of Job shows us there is no comfort or healing in playing the blame game. It just makes God angry and makes us feel even worse.

The neglect or abuse of children is not God's punishment on small children for sinning against him.

Physical or learning difficulties in children are not God's punishment on bad parents.

Traumatised, troubled, truanting children are not God's punishment on adoptive families.

Whether tiny vulnerable children or active compassionate Christians, nobody is immune from suffering the long-term consequences of living in a world broken by sin.

Instead of philosophising about the suffering, Jesus models to us the alternative: choosing to walk with those who suffer, even though it means a life of suffering ourselves.

Foster care and adoption is not just a 'Bed and Breakfast' service for children, it is about voluntary redemptive suffering on behalf of children who have been traumatised.

What if Baby P had been resuscitated by the paramedics who arrived that August morning while his mother was refusing to leave for the hospital without her cigarettes?[6] What if after receiving hospital care he was fostered and then adopted? How would his physical and emotional trauma have affected him in the long term? What kinds of challenges would he have faced growing up with the memories and the knowledge of how his parents had treated him? What kind of additional parenting skills would his foster and adoptive parents have needed to help him deal with all that had happened to him? What kind of help would those foster and adoptive parents have needed to receive from their friends and family or maybe even their church?

Children who have been through even a fraction of what Baby Peter went through have experienced something called 'traumatic' or 'toxic' parenting.[7] Traditional parenting isn't going to be enough to bring healing in these situations. Experts call on foster carers and adopters to learn a whole new set of skills to practise what has been called 'therapeutic parenting' or 'therapeutic reparenting'.[8]

Imagine you are walking down the road with your family when a large dog walks past and snarls, scaring your adopted four-year-old. He jumps away and runs into the road, where he narrowly escapes being hit by a car.

A typical instinctive reaction to this would be to shout at your son. 'Get out of the road. Come here. Never jump into oncoming traffic. You frightened me and you nearly got yourself killed.'

A typical child would cope well with this reaction. It has appealed to their inbuilt sense of shame ('you frightened me') and their sense of self-preservation ('you nearly got yourself killed'). As the situation naturally diffuses and returns to equilibrium, the parent might use the incident to teach their child about the Green Cross Code, and all is well.

A traumatised child would not cope well with this reaction at all. Their sense of shame and self-preservation is likely to be missing or immature due to lack of nurture from birth. All they hear is shouting. So first they have been frightened by the dog, then by the car, then by the parent figure. It is a pattern they are all too familiar with and affirms what they already believe – that the world is a dangerous place, whatever they do. The overwhelming emotional overload may have reminded them of previous traumas and tricked the child's body into the flight response. Any attempts at comfort are likely to be rejected. Any lesson in road safety at the end of all that would not be assimilated at all.

A different reaction is called for. Therapeutic parenting calls for the parent figure to remain calm, diffuse the situation quickly and help the child to return to an equilibrium. At that point it may be helpful to say something like, 'Thank goodness you are all right. It was okay to be scared by the dog, and your body told you to run. Shall we go home now or go to the park?'

This reaction goes against the grain. But by managing our own emotions, we can help a child to manage theirs. By affirming that we believe the child's safety is important

('Thank goodness you are all right'), that their reaction was understood ('It was okay to be scared'), and giving back some control with a choice ('Shall we go home now or go to the park?'), we can use difficult situations to help us in our job of rebuilding a child's stress-management and self-esteem. The lesson in road safety can wait.

Adoptive mum Grace Harris tells the story of a girl who continually stole from her foster family. Stealing and shoplifting is a common problem for adopted teens who often subconsciously feel that their families have been stolen from them. In this case, the mother sat down with the foster child and explained why stealing was unacceptable. Then she presented the child with her most treasured necklace and locket and asked the child to keep it safe for her.[9]

These are examples of therapeutic parenting. It involves putting yourself in the shoes of the child and looking at the deeper issues behind the behaviour. In the second case, the mum understood that the stealing was a symptom of her foster daughter's need for security, and addressed it by tangibly assuring her that she was committed to a long-term trusting relationship with her.

I have met many adoptive parents who have seen slow but sure change in their traumatised children's ability to cope with family life. The rewards can be incredibly fulfilling for both parent and child.

I have also met many adoptive parents who are exhausted from managing their own and their children's emotions, from thinking of creative solutions to everyday issues, from trying to contain negative behaviour to within the home and from wondering about all the 'if only' questions that harangue them. If only I knew what my child was reliving. If only I could have had him from a younger age. If only I could take away the pain my child is experiencing. If only I knew that tomorrow it would all be better. If only God would sort this all out now.

After Job has asked many questions, and his so-called friends have asked a whole lot more, finally it is God's turn to speak. God gives no explanations. God gives no answers.

On the contrary, God asks more questions. Over sixty more.

These unanswered and unanswerable questions point to the majesty of God and finitude of human existence as parameters for the whole problem of suffering, and are an encouragement to keep on believing and trusting no matter what. From these questions God helps us see that he is firmly in control.

The God who brought the sky, the sea and the earth into being is big enough to deal with the challenges of our lives.

The God who can feed lions and ravens and directs the flight of the hawk is wise enough to work out justice for the earth.

The God who commands the constellations and designs sea creatures has the skill to help us navigate every possible challenge we will ever face.

The God who controls the light and the darkness will

one day reveal the mystery of why the innocent suffer while he watches.

The God who calls lightning strikes to account will also one day call those who sinned against Baby Peter to account.

The God who brought the universe into being will usher in a new kingdom where there will be no more suffering, no more abuse, no more pain.

The God who allowed his Son to die on the cross for us calls us to take up our cross, and promises to meet us, preserve and sustain us through our pain.

FOR FURTHER CONSIDERATION

Could you foster or adopt a traumatised child? Therapeutic parenting is complex and you may need professional help. But don't be put off because this help is available and anyone can learn. Here are ten things traumatised children would want you to be. How can you begin practising these skills?

1. Someone who will listen to them.
2. Someone who will spend time with them and give them eye-contact.
3. Someone who will fill in the gaps of their childhoods, whether that is doing a puzzle or sitting on the beach or teaching them to ride a bike or swim.

4. Someone who will fight for their rights.

5. Someone who will model appropriate behaviour, but not expect it immediately

6. Someone whom they can trust not to use coercion, threats or physical means of discipline.

7. Someone who shows that there is lots to smile and laugh about.

8. Someone who is unshockable.

9. Someone who is willing to be a teacher and a learner, and is able to look for creative solutions.

10. Someone who helps them feel valued and loved, no matter what.

You can still be these things to children in care, even if you are unable to adopt or foster. How could you use these skills to support a friend, family member or church member?

SIMON AND MARIANNE'S STORY

Jesus ministered in chaos. People were shouting for him to take their sides in family feuds, washing his feet with their hair, and shouting inappropriate blessings.

Not unlike an average Sunday morning with our adopted children.

Before Children (BC), church was safe. That changed when they arrived. Only one and two years old at placement, but already full of fear, anxiety and stress. People did not understand. The well-meaning but mistaken words 'They are too young to remember anything' and 'All they need is love' made us weary of trying to explain the challenges children who've been in care face in establishing true attachment.

We decided that we would attend a very large church, and go as and when we could. We wanted to be inconspicuous, and did not want to commit. We were in retreat.

God had other plans! Through a friend of a friend a

new church found us. We were brought back into a church family. Our leaders committed to knowing us. They met with us regularly to ask how they could minister to us all. As our son David matures, his special needs have become evident, and he requires support to just attend Sunday school. His behaviour can be aggressive, 'hyper' and impulsive, and an adult is needed to regulate him. He has thrown drinks at the worship band, smashed windows and shouted obscenities.

But in this post-children phase of our life we call AD (After David), our church has been great. Once they sent the entire leadership around to pray and encourage us hours after we texted despair to them. Once they took our son off our hands for the day when he smashed the French windows in. We have a pastor who says, 'The day the church does not lovingly accept your children is the day I leave this church.'

Ministry is messy. The early Church worked within disorder and noise. Churches should be that way! Your church may not like the din, the breakages, the language. But when initial reactions turn into responses, you can trust your church to embrace your child.

CHAPTER 6

WHY CARING ABOUT WORSHIP MEANS WORSHIP BY CARING

The Scowl speaks volumes. It says, 'Be quiet because I can't worship God with this kind of commotion.'

The Furrowed Brow joins in. It says, 'What sort of parents are you that you can't keep your own children under control?'

The Tut agrees. 'They should have sent you on more training courses before they allowed you to become a foster/adoptive parent – you haven't a clue.'

Then, like a nail in the coffin of both the child and the parent's self-esteem, comes the Pity Look. It says, 'Bad luck that your family got such a raw deal.'

I have spoken to several foster and adoptive parents who have experienced these sorts of subtle messages at their local church on Sunday mornings. Some walked out and never returned.

Sunday mornings can be one of the hardest times of the week for adopted and foster families. There has already probably been an awkward discussion with the social worker about whether the child has been given the go ahead from birth parents to be taken to church services. If the children are old enough, there may have been some conversation with them too about whether they would like to come and what to expect.

Once clearance has been given and an agreement reached, then the practicalities need sorting: 'It's my turn to use the shower first.' 'Has anyone seen my red shirt?' 'Don't spill the porridge on your clean clothes.' 'Where are my house keys?'

With additional practical, medical or emotional needs to consider, a military logistics officer could be defeated by the scale of operation needed to get a blended family safely and happily to a church service on time. Sometimes they seem to succeed where a general might have failed.

Then as the service kicks off one of the kids loses it. Maybe they are emotionally drained by all the new people they have just met. Maybe it is the inability to sit still. Maybe a loud noise triggered a hyperactive fight-or-flight response. Maybe it is seeing the cross look from the other side of the room when the tin of crayons fell to the floor. Maybe a smell or a word or a stare suddenly brought back an unwanted memory. Maybe a closed door made them feel claustrophobic. Maybe an open door made them feel insecure.

Imagine this situation. You know that your two-year-old foster son spent several months in survival mode prior to his being removed. As a result he gets anxious around food. Nobody else really understands, although you have tried to explain. He sees a child on the row in front of him enjoying a snack, and his whole being still cries out that he needs that biscuit. He screams as loudly as he can, lashing out and refusing to be comforted.

You know that punishment will only reinforce the panic mode that he is in. So you try to reassure him through the tantrum. But other parents in church see only what they have been taught – he is being naughty, and you are not disciplining him.

There is nothing for it. Parent and child must run the gauntlet of disapproval and leave the service – just like the week before, and the week before that; just like most weeks.

Or should they? The Prophet Isaiah forces us to seriously reconsider our priorities:

> Stop bringing meaningless offerings!
>   Your incense is detestable to me.
> New Moons, Sabbaths and convocations –
>   I cannot bear your evil assemblies.
> Your New Moon feasts and your appointed festivals
>   I hate with all my being.
> They have become a burden to me;
>   I am weary of bearing them.
> When you spread out your hands in prayer,
>   I will hide my eyes from you;
> Even if you offer many prayers,
>   I am not listening.
>
> Your hands are full of blood!

Wash and make yourselves clean.
> Take your evil deeds out of my sight;
> stop doing wrong.
Learn to do right; seek justice.
> Defend the oppressed.
Take up the cause of the fatherless;
> plead the case of the widow.
(Isaiah 1:13–17)

Is God really asking his people to close down their worship services? Does he really hate the celebrations? Is he really telling people not to bother coming to church? Is he really saying that prayer is pointless?

Look at your church calendar. Now delete Christmas, Easter, home groups, retreats, prayer meetings and communion. Sack the church band. Tell the preacher to look for another job. Really?

What are we doing wrong?

I don't think I have ever been to a church that didn't have a music rota, a preaching slot, a collection and a prayer meeting. But I have been to plenty of churches where no one is doing anything about caring for the at-risk families, the winter shut-ins, the homeless, or those in half-way houses, children's homes, nursing homes, refuges or prisons. Isaiah's prophecy challenges us. He says we have our priorities upside down.

It is not that God doesn't want offerings – he commanded

them. It is not that God isn't interested in prayer – he initiated the conversation. It is not that God doesn't enjoy festivals – he invented them.

But none of these things are at the heart of worship.

God doesn't make it complicated. In fact he clearly summarises genuine worship in six short unequivocal headlines.

1. Stop doing wrong.
2. Learn to do right.
3. Seek justice.
4. Defend the oppressed.
5. Take up the cause of the fatherless.
6. Plead the case of the widow.

This is the kind of worship that God wants from his people. All the singing, hand-raising, festival-going in the world won't replace it. God would rather we shut down our services than carry on with them while neglecting these six headlines.

Most churches are pretty good at teaching headline number one: 'Stop doing wrong.' Some churches aren't bad at teaching headline number two either: 'Learn to do right.' But then it quickly fizzles out. Numbers three to six don't get much of a look-in.

These six headline commands don't sound like worship to us any more. They sound like hard work. They sound time-consuming. They sound energy-draining.

I usually hear worship described as just the opposite. Worship nowadays is often synonymous with relaxing in the presence of God. It is taking time out to 'just be'. It is 'me time with God'. It is being recharged by God's Spirit. It is emptying my mind of fears and concerns. It is 'waiting' on God.

Not according to Isaiah. Isaiah says if we care about worship, we should worship by caring.

It is not one or the other. Some of us buy into the passive reflective worship described above, and get so busy focusing on the one we serve and love that we forget to get round to actually serving him. Some of us buy into activism that means we are so busy doing stuff and serving God's agenda that we don't stop to reflect on who we are doing it for.

Isaiah calls us to an intimate activism and an active intimacy.

Our reflective worship services need to go hand in hand with active worship service. If one is missing, the other may as well close up shop and go home.

Active and intimate – together.

Just like God himself.

In chapter 1, we see God active: warning, punishing, delivering, purging, restoring. He is determined, dynamic, demanding, driving. Passionate.

Later in the prophecy we see the flipside: God desiring intimacy with us – gentle, patient, tender, nurturing. Compassionate. In chapter 40 we see how God

tends his flock like a shepherd:
he gathers the lambs in his arms
and carries them close to his heart;
he gently leads those that have young.
(Isaiah 40:11)

Intimate and active, God loves us and leads us. One without the other is a mockery. A true relationship with God requires us to enjoy his presence and enjoy his purposes, committing ourselves to his plans, sharing both his passion and compassion with others.

As we saw in Isaiah 58, the same idea crops up, and this time the prophet takes aim at the hypocrisy of fasting. One of the most difficult and costly spiritual disciplines, God declares it meaningless without its accompanying acts of service to the vulnerable.

Religious observance, spiritual disciplines and Christian piety can be an excuse to fill up our time with things that steer us away from doing the things that God wants from us. They can be a way to shut our eyes to the needs of the world. Instead of engagement, they can be escapism.

Caring for vulnerable children in our country is by no means the only way we can fight injustice, feed the hungry, shelter the homeless or clothe the naked. But this is a powerful, personal and profound way we can be involved in worshipping God right in our own homes.

Worship works when we provide even the most basic of needs for the most vulnerable in society. God is so closely connected to the poor that when you help them you are helping him.

Imagine my son fell off his bicycle and was injured outside your house. You rush out to help him, mop up his wounds, comfort his bruised ego, offer him something sugary to drink, and then drive him home to me. Words cannot express how grateful I am. A bond of friendship and trust is cemented between us. We are forever connected through this intimate, extra-mile kindness you have performed.

Imagine my son fell off his bicycle and was injured outside your house. You rush to pick up the phone, and leave a message expressing the depth of our friendship. You send me a Facebook message about how much you appreciate my book. You text me to say you are planning to visit. My son, still injured, lies outside your house, and when I find out I am incensed. Whatever friendship we had between us is over.

By sharing in the responsibility to protect and provide for the vulnerable, we build a bond of friendship with God, father to the fatherless. Whatever we do to offer help, shelter, food, clothing, comfort and love to those in need is worship to him.

The strong language of Isaiah is no accident. We are often too eager to pass our own verdicts on our worship experiences. But our worship is not for us. It is for God. It is God's verdict that matters. When he uses words like 'hate', 'detest', 'take no pleasure', 'cannot bear', then we must stop and listen.

Isaiah's wake-up call forces us to re-evaluate our worship.

Do we invite strangers in? Are the poor among us? Are widows and orphans provided for in our congregations, parishes and communities? Are hurting children supported?

Or are they shushed and shunned? The two-year-old having a meltdown over a biscuit. The fourteen-year-old with a shoplifting problem. The ten-year-old who can't give eye contact. The six-year-old who won't share. The eight-year-old who has to be the centre of attention.

If they are part of our church community it is a good sign. Including such as these authenticates our worship, cements our relationship with the Father to the fatherless and draws others to him.

Viv was seven years old when his father died. His uncle delivered the news of his death to him and his brother as they sat in the sunlit garden of a children's home, and their mother lay in hospital many miles away. She recovered for a time, but three years later social services came to take them away again. This time they ended up outside the door of a smiling, round-faced woman who welcomed them in with a meal of egg and chips. It felt safe and normal. Egg and chips, a house with a bath, a sense of order and a house that was cleaned regularly seemed wonderful to Viv. He describes his foster parents as 'faithful, ordinary, brilliant'. And then there was church.

> I was not ready for their church. Occasionally, I sang in
> my Anglican church choir but this did not prepare me

for the Pentecostals. It was very strange. The jolly 'Pastor' played a piano accordion accompanying himself as he sang solos from the pulpit. Between verses he would pull out a trumpet and blow. For a ten-year-old boy this was side-splittingly fun. Yet, for all the cultural oddity the people were great. There was something there I had not felt before. These people were unassuming lovers of God. There was a mix of joy, humanity, some new mates all mixed up with some really . . . really nice girls. Somehow, I got the core message of these people. It did not come directly through my foster parents, it also came through the community of which they were a part. After a while I got it that God loved me, and the cross and resurrection of Jesus proved it. This has transformed – and continues to transform – my life.[1]

John and Jilly are foster carers for particularly traumatised teenagers. They have crises and emergencies in their household on a daily basis. As a result their birth children used regularly to be standing outside music lessons, sports practice or youth groups, waiting for their parents to pick them up, wondering if they would ever arrive. Not any more. Two families in their church have assigned themselves as 'plan B' families. They have given their mobile numbers to the birth children with the invitation, 'Whatever time of day or night, if you are stuck somewhere and you need a lift or some help we will drop whatever we are doing and come up and get you.'

Children like Viv, and like those cared for by John and Jilly, discover not only a family committed to therapeutic parenting, but an extended family in the church equally committed to nurturing the kids. Imagine that there were at least one adoptive or foster family in every church in the country. That would end the waiting for the majority of kids in the system. But it may not only be an end – it may be the beginning of a chain reaction.

As Donna, mother of two, grieved the death of her own mother, she began to think about what it was like for young children who lost their parents. She sensed a call to adopt and approached a local agency. She was shocked to find out how many kids there were waiting, and eventually adopted four children from very troubled backgrounds, doubling the size of her family.

Donna's church was a small community church of ordinary people whose aim was to 'get through life one day at a time' and impact their community and their world 'one heart at a time'. As the church embraced the challenge of helping to care for and nurture Donna's adopted children, they also embraced her vision. Twenty other families decided that they too would adopt, then twenty more, and so far the congregation has adopted seventy-seven children.[2]

The main challenges facing the care system are recruiting and supporting carers, and then supporting the children in the placements and ensuring that they don't break down.

If every church in the country supported one adoptive/foster family through their application and placement, we would potentially increase the chance of that placement working.

Imagine the impact that each church, made up of one carer family and lots of supporters, could have.

The child who thought nobody cared about him would have a whole community willing to go to great lengths to show him he was valued. This would speed up his healing process and give him the best possible chance of recovery.

The carers would be buoyed up at times when they need extra time, extra resources, extra prayer. Breakdowns or disruptions would be reduced.

The system would not be filled to bursting point, because there would be people queuing up to take on even the most challenging of placements.

What a fantastic witness to the whole country!

Beginning this journey of turning your church into a missional community where foster and adoptive children and blended families can find hope and healing is easier than you might first think.

The Smile speaks volumes. It says, 'You are welcome here.'

The Compliment joins in. It says, 'There's something about you that I value.'

The Simple Kindness agrees. 'I take pleasure in offering you a drink, a listening ear, a seat beside me, a space to let off steam.'

The Radical Hospitality joins in. It says, 'Maybe I could follow your footsteps and use my home for good.'

FOR FURTHER CONSIDERATION

Is there one person or family in your church you could support to become foster or adoptive parents? What would this look like in practice? Here are ten questions to help think this through.

1. What do you imagine to be the five most difficult things about bringing foster children to the current configuration of Sunday morning worship? What could you do to help change them?
2. In your worship gatherings, how can you balance a sense of reverence with a place where children, and especially traumatised children, can feel comfortable?
3. Church pastors are busy people. How could you support them to capture and pass on a vision for caring for widows and orphans?
4. What changes might we need to make so that our Sunday schools are made ready to receive children from the care system?
5. What would need to be different on Mother's Day, Father's Day and other family occasions to make adoptive and foster children and their families more comfortable?
6. How can we make sure that foster children are included in the party invitations and play dates?

7. Does your church organise a meals rota for a family when a baby is born? Could this be extended to include the arrival of an adopted child? Are there other practical support ideas you could initiate: 'plan B' families, or approving respite carers for specific children?

8. 'Parents and carers are reminded that there is a family walk organised . . .' What difference do the words 'and carers' make to notices like these?

9. How can we prepare ourselves to be 'unshockable'? Whether it is the language used by a foster kid, or a disclosure we need to attend to, how can we avoid being seen to be judgemental?

10. How can you show genuine interest to carers in your church, without asking them questions about a child's background or current care plan that is confidential, or without the child overhearing?

GRAN AND GRANDAD'S STORY

It is a day seared in our memories. We stood on the driveway of our daughter's house as one of our grandchildren was driven away in the back of the social worker's car. Only that morning, after a long and tense court case, the judge announced his decision that Sam and his smaller sister Lucy be placed for adoption. Even the seasoned social worker – a Christian too – found it profoundly distressing: later she told us that after pulling away from the house she stopped round the corner for a good cry.

But we had little time for tears until later. Within the hour we were meeting Sam and Lucy's older siblings from school, faced with the unenviable task of telling them their younger brother would not be waiting for them back at home that day or any other day.

Lucy, who had already been in foster care for a year, was also placed for adoption that day. For us, contact continued with Sam and Lucy through their wonderful foster parents for a few short months until suitable adoptive parents were found. Then our visits came to an end.

How do we feel? As grandparents? As Christians?

As grandparents, it has often been like a runaway roller coaster in which everyone except us determines the twists and turns, the ups and downs, the high-speed bursts of activity and the times of nervous waiting while nothing happens. The professionals, the parents, the experts, the courts all have their say, but we can only look on. We don't get to write reports; we don't get our day in court. The parents have multiple chances to change the situation but don't . . . or won't . . . or just can't. The only power available to us is prayer.

But at the same time, we are often the first port of call for help. Sam and Lucy's older siblings regularly stay with us: we try to show them a different way of life. We do far more than many grandparents should: making up last-minute Christmas stockings when none had materialised at home is one sad example, hiring a minibus to take them and their cousins for a week's holiday a happier one.

We drive several thousand miles a year to pick them up and drop them off – often returning to scenes of chaos which bring them and us down to earth with a bump. Sometimes we are the uncomfortable bridge between the family and the professionals. Could we smooth this over? Could we get the children to this or that appointment? Sometimes we are tired, occasionally angry, often disappointed, frequently frustrated, but always 'there'.

As Christians, we remind ourselves that God's love is agape love: a love that seeks the best for others, even at deep personal cost, a love that lets go and doesn't take control. God's love for the world is such that he let go of his own beloved Child for the sake of others.

Was the judge's decision right? Absolutely, but we have lost our grandchildren through no fault of our own. Apart from a hoped-for annual exchange of letters and photos, there is no contact. Might they one day be brought back to us, a kind of resurrection? We simply don't know. Like Hannah who let go and entrusted her God-given child Samuel to God's keeping, we can do nothing less – and nothing greater – for our grandchildren.

CHAPTER 7

WHY WE ARE CALLED TO HOLD ON
AND LET GO

There's something bittersweet about the photos on our mantelpiece. Each child we have fostered has a place of honour there. Their portraits remind me of giggles with bubbles in the garden, splashing on the beach, picnics in the park, or birthday parties with cake and ice cream. Happy moments etched into my memory and my heart. But each beaming face also reminds me of children who are no longer with us. Some have been adopted, others have been reunited with parents. Each one has left a loss and a hole in our family.

When other people look at these photos there is one response that crops up over and over again.

'I could never do what you do – I would love them too much to be able to ever let them go.'

They may think they are paying my family a veiled compliment, but all I hear is a veiled criticism of my emotional capacity.

I bite my lip. Self-doubt is an occupational hazard for

a carer. Did I love them enough? Did I fight for them hard enough? Did I do right by them? Do I miss them enough?

Then I bite my tongue.

They think they would love too much?

So they do nothing.

What kind of love is so worried about getting hurt that it doesn't get involved at all?

Being realistic about the emotional impact of saying goodbye to foster children is important. But for some people their own fear of pain stops them getting involved with kids in care. When there are children who desperately need a safe place to live and emotional investment, should our first question really be, 'Can I cope with my own personal heartache?'

Imagine God thought like that. Would he have committed to a relationship with us?

I grieve over every child who leaves. Strangely, that grief begins the moment they arrive. As I hear their stories and find ways to connect with them by sharing eye contact or a bowl of crisps or a smile, an emotional connection is built that will one day be the cause of pain. That grief hangs around in the background over the weeks, months or years that the children stay with us. It lingers ominously as we do ordinary things like eat breakfast together, go shopping together or read bedtime stories together. Every photo I take of a giggling foster child reminds me that one day they will be gone. And then one day they are gone. Sometimes that grief hurts so much it makes me want to quit.

But my grief is a small price to pay for the potential of seeing a child flourish. It is also a small price to pay to identify with our Father God who has grieved over each one of us and loved us anyway.

The book of Hosea tackles exactly that dilemma. God was fully aware of what he was getting into. Israel's rebellion did not take him by surprise, but that did not stop God from emotionally investing in his people. God knew he would be abandoned and betrayed by his sinful people, but he chose to love them anyway.

Being emotionally distant would be so much easier. There would be far less grief and pain. But God, contrary to popular opinion, does not stand in a celestial pulpit six (billion) feet above contradiction issuing commands from on high, unaffected by our struggles and troubles.

Hosea is the book of the Bible that most clearly refutes that perception of God. It is a story that famously involves the disastrous family life of the prophet. His wife Gomer is unfaithful to him, but Hosea is called by God to go and find her again, renew his affection for her, and restore his marriage.

Anyone who has experienced marital breakdown or the betrayal of a friend or family member will empathise a little with the pain that Hosea experienced. And this is the point. God says this is how he feels too. God is the innocent party in a marriage breakdown between him and his people.

And, like Hosea, God knew it would happen when he made the vows.

If the pain of a betrayal of a marriage isn't emotionally powerful enough to convey the extent of emotional investment that God has poured into his people, God introduces another metaphor in Hosea chapter 11. He now compares his distress over his people to that of a father losing a son.

We are on hallowed ground in these pages as God reports in the first person. It almost feels like we are eavesdropping as God flicks through a family photo album of his son, Israel, sometimes referred to by his pet name Ephraim, in the wake of his grief. Listen to how God reminisces in very personal terms.

'There's a picture of little Israel learning to walk.'
'Look at this one of Israel getting fixed up after a fall.'
'Here's another one of Israel being fed.'
You get the picture?

> When Israel was a child, I loved him,
>   and out of Egypt I called my son.
> But the more they were called,
>   the more they went from me.
> They sacrificed to the Baals
>   and they burned incense to images.
> It was I who taught Ephraim to walk,
>   taking them by the arms;

111

but they did not realise
   it was I who healed them.
I led them with cords of human kindness,
   with ties of love.
To them I was like one who lifts
   a little child to the cheek,
   and I bent down to feed them . . .
How can I give you up, Ephraim?
   How can I hand you over, Israel?
How can I treat you like Admah?
   How can I make you like Zeboyim?
(Hosea 11:1–4, 8)

God is a hands-on dad. He has not outsourced the raising of his children to their mother or grandparents or a nursery or a nanny. He did not miss the crucial milestones of their development so far. He intertwines vignettes from the story of the nation of Israel – their rescue from Egypt, their rebellion and turning to other gods – with his affectionate, involved parenting: 'It was I who taught Ephraim to walk, taking them by the arms . . . I who healed them. I led them with cords of human kindness . . . I bent down to feed them.'

I have loved helping to teach my foster children how to walk, fondly holding out my arms as they stumble their way to me. One was so desperate that he lurched across the room before he could even balance himself. One was so disabled that it took years of physiotherapy and cajoling and a walking aid before she would even stand up. One would rather shuffle along on her bottom than risk falling. Another had every neighbour on our cul-de-sac practising with her up and down the road, when my back was almost permanently reshaped from her determination.

There's no doubt these experiences bonded us together. I still remember the feeling of their hands squeezing mine as they clung on for dear life. I have indelibly imprinted on my brain their beaming faces as they work out that putting one foot in front of the other accelerates them from one side of the room to the other.

I'll never forget coming home from work after a dreary board meeting in a stuffy room and heading straight for the park with our foster son where, in twenty minutes, he went from never having got on a bike to pedalling full pelt, with his shouts of 'Awesome! Awesome!' echoing around the play area.

That was the highlight of my day and sharing that moment connected us together. I have a photograph that captures his utter joy.

Another bittersweet photograph for my collection.

These experiences make passing the children on more difficult. Each day we grow closer together we grow closer to the day when they will be taken from us.

Some people ask if it is better to remain aloof, holding back emotions to protect your heart and making it easier to facilitate any transition. The answer is emphatically no.

Emotional investment is part and parcel of any parent's role.

This relational bonding that takes place between parent and child is vital for a child's sense of well-being. Over time it is built by shared experiences, smiles, eye contact, sharing emotions, taking pleasure in the child, giving praise, setting boundaries and coming through with what is promised. Most children take these foundational building blocks for granted. Most children in care need additional help to rebuild these missing connections.

The experts call this *attachment*.

Hosea calls it 'cords of human kindness' and 'ties of love'.

Giving a child the skill of making attachments is even more important than teaching them to walk or ride a bike. It teaches them how to trust, how to love, how to connect with others. I would rather lose my legs than lose the ability to have relationships. Teaching the skill of relationship building cannot be done through sticking on a DVD or sending the child to school. It can only be done through bonding with the child. If it doesn't hurt when a foster child leaves our family then we have done something wrong. If it doesn't feel like our hearts have been ripped out of our chests when the social worker or adoptive parents drive off, then we have failed that child.

God knows the excruciating pain of this kind of separation.

'How can I give you up, Ephraim? How can I hand you over, Israel?'

Of course, Israel wasn't taken away by court order to an adoptive family or returned to their parents. Israel walked away from God in rebellion.

This can happen in any family. Your children may choose to shut you out emotionally, or walk out on the family you have worked hard to build, or turn their backs on their spiritual family. It is a common enough story.

God knows what it is like to lose a child. This wasn't the first time.

The opening chapters of the Bible describe God creating the universe. Just like a parent meticulously preparing a nursery with mobiles and furniture and murals, God hung the stars in the sky, sculpted the mountains and rivers and brought the landscape alive by adding birds and fish. Everything was ready. The world contained all that a beloved son or daughter could possibly need. The only thing missing was the child. So God creates human beings to enjoy all that he has prepared for them. But only a few chapters later, we already read about human rebellion. The relationship is spoilt almost immediately because of sin.

From Genesis to Hosea we see a pattern of gracious loving investment from God, and heartless, ungrateful rejection from his people. The book of Judges, for example, reads like a broken record. A seemingly unending cycle of God's people needing rescue, then a brief period of respite, during which they again forget about God and rebel against him. God has to send retribution before they realise they need to repent and ask him again to intervene.

Rescue. Respite. Rebellion. Retribution. Repentance. Rescue. Respite. Rebellion. Retribution. Repentance. Rescue.

Over and over again in the book of Judges. Over and over again in the history of God's people. Over and over again in my own life.

God did not stay away from us, despite knowing that we would fail him and betray him time and again. Despite the heartache that came with a relationship with us, God poured his love and forgiveness into our lives.

Why? Because we were spiritual orphans, and it is in God's nature to care: 'For in you the fatherless find compassion' (Hosea 14:3).

This is wonderfully and poetically expounded as God goes on to describe his commitment to his lost child.

> I will heal their waywardness
>> and love them freely,
>>> for my anger has turned away from them.
> I will be like the dew to Israel;
>> he will blossom like a lily.
> Like a cedar of Lebanon
>> he will send down his roots;
>>> his young shoots will grow.
> His splendour will be like an olive tree,
>> his fragrance like a cedar of Lebanon.

People will dwell again in his shade;
  they will flourish like the corn,
they will blossom like the vine –
  Israel's fame will be like the wine of Lebanon.
Ephraim, what more have I to do with idols?
  I will answer him and care for him.
I am like a flourishing juniper;
  your fruitfulness comes from me.
(Hosea 14:4–8)

God sees past the rebellion and the betrayal and the heart-ache to the potential, and instead of holding back on his love, pours even more into the relationship.

This is the grace each one of us has received. This is the grace each one of us has the power to pass on.

'I could never let a child go – I would love them too much.' This is the most common reason I come across for why Christians say that they won't consider fostering. But surely we are clearly taught to put the needs of others above our own needs, and that especially applies to the most vulnerable in our society.

'I am not sure that I could love a child that wasn't mine.' This is the second most commonly stated reason Christians give for not considering fostering, and one I was guilty of holding onto for a while. As we share our concerns while walking our dogs, or stroking our cats, the irony, the fallacy, the absurdity stares us in the face. My O level in biology may have been a long time ago, but as far as I know humans are not yet able to birth animals. How come we have no problem effortlessly and unquestioningly showering love and affection on our pets who we have no biological connection with, but many of us believe we couldn't love a child we haven't given birth to?

Besides, love is not an automatic by-product of biology anyway. Love is a choice. We choose to love our genetically unrelated spouses, their families, our pets. And we choose to love our foster children and adopted children. They won't all be as cute and polite as Anne of Green Gables. They won't all be as cuddly as Paddington Bear. They won't all be as adorable as the three little sisters in the brilliant film *Despicable Me*. They all come with their ready-made personalities and a range of flaws and foibles and habits and needs. However damaged or dysfunctional they are, we can still choose to love them.

God sees how far short we fall of his standards and how broken and damaged we are, and how highly likely we are to let him down, yet he still chooses to shower his perfect love on us. Love is his choice.

God calls Christians to follow his example, to tap into his resources, and to choose unconditional love for everyone: our husbands, our wives, our church family, our neighbours, even our enemies. If we are not willing to make this choice, then we are told pretty clearly that we don't belong to God (1 John 3:16–20).

We choose to love because God first chose to love us.

We choose to risk our love on broken children with all

the potential for both intense pain and incredible blessing because that is how God first chose to love us.

Elizabeth made this choice for the sake of a baby with a sweet nature, sparkly eyes and sensitive airways. She had been running a small charity that arranged foster care, support and education for vulnerable children in Mozambique, a country where neighbours invariably step in to try and help when children are orphaned, despite being impoverished themselves, and Elizabeth sensed an implicit challenge. As far as her Christian faith was concerned, she had felt for a long time that it was 'all talk and no trousers'. She was tired of just talking the talk in groups and on Sundays, and she had this strong urge that if she didn't do it, who would?

After a two-year process to get approved, a gorgeous five-month-old baby girl joined Elizabeth's own birth children and was part of their family for ten happy months. When she moved on for adoption, the whole family experienced a huge roller coaster of emotions and exhaustion. In Elizabeth's words, it was 'a bittersweet journey of indescribable joy and love and yet loss, pain and sadness'. Why on earth would anyone choose this?

Elizabeth said:

> If we don't do these things as Christians, who are we? Fostering so far has been by far the hardest thing I have done and yet the most rewarding, redemptive and inspiring. I have been aware of my own weaknesses and

failures so much more and have been pushed out of my comfort zone, but it has given me life, in the truest sense of the word, in all its fullness. Who knows what the next part of the journey will bring?[1]

FOR FURTHER CONSIDERATION

How much do we emotionally invest in the children around us? Think about your birth children, grandchildren, nephews and nieces, neighbourhood kids and church kids and ask yourself the following questions. How can you improve in these areas in order to help build positive qualities in 'your' children?

1. How much eye contact do you give your children?
2. How much quality and quantity of time do you spend with your children?
3. How well do you know what happens in the daily lives of your children?
4. How easy do you find it to generate conversation with your children and move it beyond superficial levels?
5. How often do you praise your children?
6. How often do you pray for your children?
7. How often do you support the youth or children's ministries?

8. How likely are you to spot when a child is feeling down or discouraged?
9. Which child are you best placed to engage with through a shared interest or skill?
10. Which child are you best placed to mentor or disciple?

TARA'S STORY

I was two years old when I came from Korea and was joined with my new family. My mother wanted a daughter after a medical issue prevented her from having more children by birth. Her husband agreed to the adoption because he knew his marriage was in trouble and he thought I would save it.

From the beginning I bore the weight of this expectation. The failure to deliver a result brought my parents to divorce, but it also emotionally scarred me in ways that took a long time to reconcile.

Now as this adoptee lives out being an adoptive mother of her own children, I see the effects of adoption on a marriage from the other side. When my husband and I chose to adopt three children from Ethiopia after having two birth children, it wasn't for any reason other than we felt God was calling us to this journey and we wanted to obey our heavenly Father. We knew the challenges of adoption from my own experience and how it would or would not affect our marriage. We knew that it would be difficult, challenging and a journey of faith to what God called us to. We knew all too personally that we could not walk into it with a fairy-tale ending in mind. We knew that adoption was not about us being saintly, or saving lives of children, but it was simply being obedient to God's command to care for the fatherless.

One of our children has some very challenging behaviours from his life lived on the street. If we had entered into adoption with a marriage already riddled with issues it would have ultimately resulted in history repeating itself in my life. My husband and I have worked hard to keep our marriage a priority over our children from the first day I gave birth to our oldest son. Without the stability, confidence and tools in how to make and keep our marriage strong, we would not be able to withstand some of the challenges adoption can bring to a family. Our marriage has been challenged by virtue that the enemy knows if he divides us as a couple, then he wins by successfully stirring discontent and conflict in the family. He can cause stress, strain, discontentment, disagreement, division, doubt and guilt within your marriage. It has been vital that we find time for ourselves individually to rest and as a couple to connect, but even more importantly we've had to stay close to Jesus.

> *Tara Bradford is the Director of Encompass Orphan Care, a US-based organisation with a passion to empower children through adoption, foster care and strategic development.*

CHAPTER 8

WHY ADOPTING A JESUS MODEL AFFECTS WHY WE ADOPT

When we became foster parents we attended several training sessions. The one that hit home hardest was a little exercise they got us to do. Try it out for yourself:

- Write down the one place in the world that is most precious to you.
- Write down the one object in the world that is most precious to you.
- Write down the one person in the world that is most precious to you.

Help! For a start, multiple answers popped into my head. It was hard to choose my favourite place. Was it the family dinner table or the park where my kids had learned to ride their bikes, or the study with my precious collection of books? It was difficult choosing between my laptop, wedding ring, mobile phone and photo albums. And the last question was agonising. My wife, my mum, my dad, my sister? Which one of my children?

These are heart-wrenching choices. But it was about to get a lot harder. With the three most precious things to me spelled out on a piece of fresh white paper, we were given black marker pens and told that we had to choose to lose one thing from the list. It's not as easy as it sounds. Cross it out – it is lost to you and you will never see it again.

I went for the object – I would rather live without things than people and places. Note to self: stop living as though stuff matters more than people.

It's tough to imagine losing something so precious to us. But it's not over yet. Do it again. Lose one more thing from the list. Cross it out. It's gone.

This time I crossed out my most precious place. The idea of never having dinner at our kitchen table enjoying the lively happy chatter, surrounded by photos of my children when they were babies . . . What a terrible loss that would be.

Now cross out your last remaining thing. You will never see that again either.

I only had people left. Taking the pen and crossing a name off a piece of paper was surprisingly difficult for me. I know the pain of losing someone close. The idea of crossing out my children or wife or mother or father or sister, never to see them again, was unbearable.

Of course there was a point to what seemed like a manipulative exercise. None of us will have to choose those losses, but briefly those of us in the room had a window of insight into what it is like for children entering the care system, losing everything, everywhere and everyone that are important to them simultaneously. For those children who aren't traumatised before going into care, being removed into care is a trauma in itself.

One lad we looked after expressed this by continually asking when the next meal would be. Another by that heartbreaking pensive look every time my wife left the room. Another by a phobia of going in the car.

Some children are very resilient and overcome their anxieties quickly. Others take deep-seated pain and persistent problems with them into their adoptive families, who struggle to reconcile their own happiness at finally adopting with this damaged child who seems to push them away.

When Artyom[1] arrived in Moscow by plane, he was seven years old and he had in his hand a letter for the Russian Ministry of Education. It was from his adoptive mother in Tennessee explaining that he wasn't exactly what they were expecting and so they were returning him to the country where they had acquired him from in the first place. Like an unwanted birthday present, he was being returned. This extreme incidence of adoption breakdown sparked a diplomatic meltdown between Russia and America and a threat to stop all transnational adoption between the two countries.

For Artyom it was his second rejection. First he was rejected by his birth parents, then by his adopted parents. Sadly adoption breakdown happens more than it should. It is estimated that up to 9 per cent of adoptions fail in the UK, with a quarter of adoptive families 'in crisis'.[2] Hundreds of children in the UK are at risk of experiencing the double despair of losing two families.

These statistics must act as a reality check. We can't afford to go into adoption with rose-tinted glasses, imagining that a child is going to fit neatly and painlessly into our families. We must be wise about whether or not we are up for the task. We must be wise enough to understand the impact that history, ethnicity, culture, abuse and genetics will have on a child for good and for bad.

We need to be wise enough to get skilled and clued up on what to expect.

We need to be wise enough to ask our friends, families and churches to give us straight advice about whether they think we can handle it, and to be honest about the kind and amount of support they will realistically be willing to give to us. We must also be gracious enough to commit to the children in our care for better or for worse: to make the pledge that we will not return children because they don't make the grade; to do everything in our power to ensure that children receive healing under our roofs, not secondary trauma.

But these statistics must also prepare us for the worst-case scenario. However much we may feel we are prepared for our lives to be turned upside down, we must also be aware that sometimes in extreme cases adoptions do not work. What would you do if you found one adopted child sexually abusing another? What would you do if they set the house on fire, not once, but twice? Serious thought would have to go into what is the best course of action for these children. For Christians who have had adoptions fail in these sort of circumstances not only can they feel they have let the child down, the family down and themselves down, there are the added pressures of feeling they have let the Church and God down.

In the moving book, *The Trouble with Alex*, author and adoptive mum Melanie Allen tells the painful story of the breakdown of her family. The dream she had of adopting a child with extra needs turned into a nightmare, as she failed to get a diagnosis or appropriate treatment for what Melanie eventually believed to be 'Reactive Attachment Disorder',[3] now a more commonly understood condition suffered by children who have been seriously neglected. Melanie is open about her mistakes as a parent, but also open about the mistakes made by the professionals involved. Although she was a caring and devoted mother to Alex, and went as far as she could to advocate for her child, eventually she had to admit defeat as her home was destroyed, the placement disrupted and her marriage also broke down.

Just as no one enters marriage expecting divorce, no one adopts expecting disruption. The Bible's teaching on divorce is clear: God hates it, but it is also a legitimate option under extreme circumstances. We can infer that God feels the same about an adoption disruption. God knows that we are broken and fallen people who live in a broken and fallen world, and as much as relationship break-down pains him, he still makes provision for it as a last resort.

As we seek to understand the feelings of loss and failure experienced by families whose adoptive placement disrupts, and the loss, displacement and bereavement that children feel, whether they have lost one family or two, we have new insight into the words of comfort Jesus spoke to his disciples in John 14.

> If you love me, you will keep my commands. And I will ask the Father, and he will give you another advocate to help you and be with you for ever – the Spirit of truth. The world cannot accept him, because it neither sees him nor knows him. But you know him, for he lives with you and will be in you. I will not leave you as orphans; I will come to you. Before long, the world will not see me any more, but you will see me. Because I live, you also will live. On that day you will realise that I am in my Father, and you are in me, and I am in you. Whoever has my commands and keeps them, he is the one who loves me. He who loves me will be loved by my Father, and I too will love them and show myself to them. (John 14:15–21)

Jesus is fully conscious of the betrayal, abandonment, injustice and agony he is going to endure on his journey to the cross,[4] but in these verses he empathises with the betrayal, abandonment and injustice the disciples are going to feel in the wake of his arrest and crucifixion.

He says, 'I will not leave you as orphans.'

For three years, home for the disciples had been wherever Jesus was. They had hiked the length and breadth of Israel with him, climbed mountains together, braved the wilderness with him and weathered storms in his company. Jesus had given them comfort, identity, protection, a sense of belonging, purpose, education and not a small amount of adventure. But now, in the middle of this rich, intimate and moving discourse that spans five chapters, Jesus has to tell them he is leaving.

Probably just teenagers, the day Jesus died the disciples found themselves disconnected from their birth families, witnesses of violence and abuse, having lost their provider and protector, afraid for their lives in a strange city, unsure of their future, defenceless and vulnerable. They were orphans.

Except they had been promised that Jesus was coming back for them.

What did Jesus mean?

Perhaps it was a hint that Jesus would be back post-resurrection. After all, he was going to spend forty more days with them. And those days would be game-changing. Death had been beaten. The resurrection proved the hope of heaven and put everything into perspective.

Or perhaps it was a hint that Jesus would be back at the end of time. This would be the culmination of history where all of us who are Christians are reunited with our Saviour and Lord, and all things are put right, and all our tears are washed away.

But I think there is more to it than that. The key is the word 'orphan'.

An orphan would not be satisfied by forty days of brief contact, instead of years of parenting. An orphan would not be satisfied by an absentee parent who showed up on their deathbed claiming they had never abandoned them. Jesus was not talking about his appearances before the ascension, or the ultimate reunion at the end of history. He was talking about the real presence and power of a Protector and Provider.

Jesus assures his disciples that he is not walking out on them, he is walking ahead of them. He is not giving up on them, he is giving them a way up to the Father's house. He is not rejecting them, he is being rejected so that they can be accepted into the family. He is dying to welcome all of us into his Father's house. Literally. We will not be left as orphans.

And these assurances are bracketed by two references to the one Jesus is promising to send to them for always – the Holy Spirit. There is a reference to the Spirit as the Advocate and Truth-holder, and a later reference to the Spirit as the Advocate and Teacher. With the Spirit present in our lives, we have access to everything Jesus gave his disciples: comfort, identity, protection, belonging, purpose, education – and not a small amount of adventure.

As Christians we gratefully receive all these blessings as

we welcome the Holy Spirit showing us the Father, and helping us be like Jesus.

We can be like Jesus not only because of the Holy Spirit's work *in* our lives, but also because of the Holy Spirit's work *through* our lives.

We too can say to those around us, 'We will not leave you as orphans.' We too can offer to those feeling abandoned comfort, identity, protection, belonging, purpose, education – and not a small amount of adventure.

Jesus models for us selfless commitment and inspires us to love to the extreme.

I have seen this selfless commitment and love to the extreme lived out by some foster parents and adoptive parents I have met who have learned to love against all odds. They have decided to stick by foster children other foster parents have turned away. They have experienced the deliberate destruction of their property, theft, physical violence against them and their children and have even had family pets assaulted. These families are trying hard to demonstrate Jesus' promise, 'We will not leave you', even to children who have suffered so much that they are struggling to know how to behave.

Most children in the care system are nowhere near as challenging as this, but a few definitely are. As part of the assessment and matching process, social workers try to take care not to place these extremely damaged children in homes where parents are going to be pushed beyond their limits to cope.

However, even children far less challenging need us to learn unrelenting, unconditional love, to demonstrate God's never-giving-up love, in the wake of losing their own parents. Being prepared to offer them love and healing is always a powerful illustration of God's grace.

For some foster and adopted children, this demonstration of God's love visibly lived out in front of them is so powerful that they not only find emotional healing, but also a spiritual purpose to their lives. For others, they seem to deliberately turn away from God despite everything.

Some Christian carers think that being like Jesus means preaching to the kids in our care with the primary aim of offering them spiritual comfort and purpose. Other Christian carers think that it is never appropriate to discuss faith issues with children, as we can be like Jesus to them in practical ways alone, by demonstrating care and unconditional love. Which is the correct approach?

I have met many people who have become Christians as a result of the love their foster parents or adoptive parents showed them. Some of their stories are recorded in this book. They didn't just hear the message of God's love, compassion and sacrifice for them, they experienced it through the care and unconditional love they received from their carers, and they chose to follow Jesus for themselves.

I have also met people who have been fostered and adopted by Christian families and attended church for many years but have rejected their parents' faith and have chosen to become agnostics and atheists. There are a lot of parents around who feel embarrassed or guilty about their child's decision.

In his most famous parable, Jesus describes God as a parent whose son has run away from home. This boy has turned his back on his family and on all the sensible parental advice he has ever been given, gone off in pursuit of the good life and ended up effectively living from hand to mouth in squalor and shame. When the red-faced renegade finally sheepishly returns, head in hands, to a warm embrace and red-carpet treatment, the other son walks away from the family in disgust.

Are we supposed to be critical of God's ability to parent his children when he paints this picture of two out of two kids choosing to walk away?

No. God humbly grants his children the freedom to accept or reject his love. In turn, we must give genuine freedom of choice to the children in our care regarding faith.

Our children, whether birth, fostered or adopted, should never be brainwashed or arm-twisted or press-ganged or emotionally manipulated or Bible-bashed into any conversion. Each child has the right and the responsibility to decide for themselves.

We may issue an invitation but never an imposition. We may celebrate when a child chooses to make a personal decision to follow Jesus for themselves, but we may never criticise if they don't.

We learn a lot about adoption from Jesus. We see how he loved his disciples as if they were his children. We see how he sacrifices his own life for the sake of his children. We see how he offers reassurance to a bunch of frightened teenagers. We see how he loves his children with a love that cannot stand to see them remaining as orphans. We see that he loves us so much, that he is willing to let us choose freely whether we reciprocate his love, or walk away from it. Jesus shows us how to hold on and how to let go.

We began this chapter with some honest reflections on transnational adoption. Transnational adoption at its worst removes the last strands of identity from a child who has already lost everything else – their cultural heritage, and their hope that a relative may come forward for them. Transnational adoption at its best offers a very powerful example of Jesus, whose love for his orphaned children crosses all cultural, ethnic and racial boundaries.

Tara went into transnational adoption with her eyes open, and is seeking to live out John 14 in a very meaningful way for the children she has adopted.

In a similar story, Miranda tells how she believes that her call to adopt came from a desire not only to follow Jesus' teaching, but also to live out the Jesus model of family. She had been living in Africa for twelve years when she decided to adopt her Xhosa daughter. For eight of those years her home had been in South Africa, a nation renowned for socio-economic divisions along racial lines. She writes:

> At the very time that my husband and I were asking ourselves whether our family was yet complete, we were

also wondering how to live with integrity in such a divided society. What does it mean to live as a follower of Jesus when I and my immediate neighbours have plenty, but a little further down the street others are living with far less? Does being a person of faith make a difference to the way I respond to this reality? Do my beliefs spill over and affect the people around me?

After much prayer, research and meeting with others who had adopted inter-racially, we decided that this was to be part of our response to those questions. Not as a 'rescue operation' but as an integration of our desire to extend our family and to live lives that, in some small way, incarnated who we believe Jesus to be.

When Angelique joined our family she was eight weeks old and Sarah, our birth daughter, was six. Coming from England, where there has been a somewhat negative attitude towards inter-racial adoptions, we thought hard about the question of raising a family of different racial origins. However, we have been consistently amazed at the positive reactions of South Africans where people seem to be instinctively conscious of the redemptive potential for racial unity that adoption offers. Whatever fears I had have been left in the wake of the incredible richness Angelique has brought to our lives. Not just because she is funny and intelligent and beautiful – and she is all these things – but because adoption is somehow an expression of God's heart.

FOR FURTHER CONSIDERATION

What does it mean to understand adoption as a 'demonstration of God's love' or an 'expression of God's heart'? How can we reflect the following aspects of Jesus' love for us in our own family lives? How would these values affect the way we do adoption, fostering and care for vulnerable children? Think of other aspects of Jesus' love that are meaningful to you and ways you could live those out for others to experience.

1. LOVE – Jesus chooses to shower affection on us despite our shortfalls.
2. GRACE – Jesus gives us what we do not deserve.
3. SACRIFICE – Jesus puts our needs above his own.
4. FREEDOM – Jesus gives us the choice to receive and reciprocate his love.
5. STICKABILITY – Jesus does not abandon us when it gets tough.
6. COMFORT – Jesus listens to our anxieties and sends a comforter.
7. REDEMPTION – Jesus extricates us from trouble and releases us from guilt.
8. DOWNWARD MOBILITY – Jesus gave up riches in heaven and chose poverty to rescue us.

9. MISSION – Jesus lived the whole of his life to please God in every area.

10. ADVOCACY – Jesus spoke up for the needs of the vulnerable.

DAVID'S STORY

I believe that adoption by indigenous families allows the adopted child to embrace their cultural and language heritage while experiencing the unconditional love and support offered by a true family. In situations where no local indigenous family can be found for a particular child, international adoptions should be welcomed with the intent to place the child into a loving family.

This is the story of one such child, my daughter Sasha, and our journey through international adoption.

She was sitting on top of the jungle gym, a sad expression behind her eyes, watching us play volleyball with the other children. She seemed interested in what we were doing, yet rather guarded. After a little coaxing, she joined the group at the Russian orphanage, crafting bracelets out of multi-coloured string. My wife Lisa sat next to her and got her smiling, and our four girls joined in the fun making bracelets, eating watermelon and playing. This was the first day we met Sasha, at an orphanage in Siberia, where we were living for an extended summer in 2005.

Over the next three years, we spent a lot of time with Sasha, during summer and winter camps, and other orphanage outreach efforts with the ministry I directed. She grew close to my family during our summer camp efforts, from cuddling up with a book on my wife's lap to spending the entire day hand in hand with my youngest at camp. At the end of the last camp, all of the orphans boarded a bus headed back to town, Sasha's hand pressed hard against the window, tears rolling down her cheeks, saying goodbye. It is a picture I will never forget.

Over the next six months, our kids kept pressing us to adopt Sasha. We shared all of the reasons it wasn't possible – we were living on a missionary salary, we already had four kids, it's so expensive to adopt internationally. Despite our protests, the questions continued. 'Why can't we adopt Sasha?' 'Let's adopt Sasha!'

During a worship service, the Lord put Sasha on my heart to the extent that I was face down weeping for her. I was not aware that at the same time, five seats to my left, Lisa was in the same position, crying for the little girl God was calling us to adopt. Our girls, aged ten to seventeen at the time, enthusiastically supported the decision, laughing and crying tears of joy at the news.

At fifteen years old, Sasha was considered an older orphan with some medical issues, and her prospects for adoption were slim. She had lived in three different orphanages over a six-year period, received very little education, and desperately needed a family. Her only remaining relatives in Russia were unable or unwilling to adopt her. She was alone. Miraculously, it took only six months to finalise the adoption.

Today is the fourth anniversary of her adoption. We love her and are thrilled that she is our daughter, and she is happy to be in a loving family that supports her. This is her anniversary message to the world: 'So, today is the day when I became part of the most wonderful family in the whole entire world. They are the most wonderful people in the whole world. I am the luckiest person in the world. I love you guys . . . I couldn't ask for a better family. Your presence has made my life so much better. And it's always going to be like this!'

David Hennessey is Director for the CAFO Global Network, Christian Alliance for Orphans.

CHAPTER 9

WHY WE HOPE TO TURN FEAR INTO HOPE

I picked up the phone at the end of a routine day at the office. The caller said, 'Is that Mr Kandiah? This is the Inland Revenue.' Talk about fear. My heart felt like it was about to check out for the rest of the day.

I don't have an offshore bank account in the Cayman Islands, and at the time I was working for a local church with three kids under the age of three so I hardly had any money in any bank account. But a phone call from the Inland Revenue was about as welcome as another hole in my head.

Thankfully my heart kept beating long enough to hear that our forthcoming drop-in debt counselling and financial management day we had organised in our church had attracted some interest and they wanted to send along some advisors to help and offer confidential advice about tax. These advisors turned out to be not dreary men with calculators and pin-stripe suits, but two larger-than-life West Indian women who had big smiles and a great sense of humour. My preloaded assumptions about HMRC couldn't have been further from the truth.

I had a similar set of prejudices around social workers before I started working with them.

My eldest son took his first steps when he was just nine months old. A couple of weeks later he managed to walk across the room and into a door and a large purple bump grew instantaneously on his forehead. A trip to the doctor reassured us that no damage had been done to him, but for weeks afterwards we feared the rumours that a trip to a doctor with a bruised child would have the dreaded repercussion of a check-up visit from a social worker and a report into our suitability as parents.

In my head social services were the enemy. They had the power to rip my family apart and take away my only son.

Even when we decided to become foster carers, we had always focused on the relationships our family would have with the foster children. It didn't really sink in just how involved our lives would become with the social work professionals, or how impacted we would be by their dedication.

Let me introduce you to some of them.

One of them has a big bunch of flowers in her hand and some sweets for our kids as we wave a teary goodbye to a little girl we have fostered for three years.

Another one spends the day with me in an African embassy basement where no phones and laptops are allowed, on an unlikely mission to get a last-minute passport.

Here's another one three hours away from home on her day off to ensure that the boy who just had to give a police interview against his parents also gets to have a fun activity weekend with us.

And there's one parked outside my house crying. He is struggling with a heavy workload and the emotional pressure of the cases he is involved with.

To be honest, social workers have one of the most difficult jobs around. Not only are they often seen by society as bad guys in the same category as tax inspectors and traffic wardens, they also face pressures at work most of us cannot imagine.

When cases like Baby P's or Victoria Climbié's hit the headlines they are harangued in the press for being inattentive, not asking enough questions, being incompetent and unable to follow straightforward child protection guidelines. The rest of the time they are often accused of being nosy and intrusive, asking too many questions and being inflexible in following child protection guidelines. They then have to sleep at night with those impossible decisions either to leave a child in a risky environment or to remove them from the only security they know.

Christians often take prejudice against social workers to a whole other level. I have met hundreds of Christians who believe that there is a bias against Christian fostering. Some focus on the perceived fear that social workers have of evangelical Christians, imagining them to be a cult who will brainwash a child and force them through religious rites. Others focus on the public position Christians have taken regarding issues of same-sex attraction, and its incompatibility with the social worker's desire for a child to be accepted whatever their sexuality.

In the light of the possibility of prejudice against us, it is entirely counter-productive to respond with prejudice or, worse, antagonism against social workers. Many, but by no means all, social workers, along with a large swathe of the UK population, have a very limited experience or under-standing of the Christian faith and so it is not surprising that we need to take some time to work through these issues and remove some misconceptions.

What any assessing social worker is trying to find out is if we are suitable parents to vulnerable children. Some Christians react to questions about why we go to church or what we believe about homosexuality as though they were being quizzed by a theology professor. They get sweaty palms and their hearts race and they insist on making sure their views and their rights are paramount. The manner and sometimes the substance of what is said can make them appear to be an unsafe place for a child who wouldn't need a lecture if they were struggling with their religious views or their sexuality.

For the majority of Christians if a child opened up about these sort of struggles, we would instinctively offer age-appropriate support in an atmosphere of acceptance and love. This is what the assessing social worker needs to know and hear. As Christians we are perfectly suited to help a child work through these issues, precisely because we believe in and have experienced ourselves the freedom to choose what we believe and how we behave, the struggles of life in a complicated and fallen world, and the overarching context of unconditional love.

Many Christians get turned down from being foster carers and adopters, as do many atheists, Muslims, agnostics and every kind of group in society. It may be their house has insufficient space, or there are queries regarding their birth children, health, ages, lack of experience, concerns raised by references, other personal issues or a perceived lack of willingness to learn or co-operate. It may be less humiliating to tell people we are turned down because we are Christians, but this only aggravates the circle of fear and suspicion which could turn the false rumour into a fact.

Many Christians are approved as foster carers and adopters, as are many atheists, Muslims, agnostics and every other kind of group in society. I have met hundreds of Christian carers. There is no bar on Christians applying to offer their homes for vulnerable children, and perhaps as Christians and the care system work more closely together the barriers will come down and the Church will become known as the place where these kids are best cared for.

Whatever our views on the possibly controversial issues, it is not hard to put them within the Christian framework of unconditional love, blessing the outsider, taking special care of the vulnerable, respecting all people equally, giving second chances again and again, wiping the slate clean, offering forgiveness, making sacrifices and showing generous hospitality. It is this powerful language that society should be hearing from us as a church, and seeing it matched with practical and selfless dedication to children in care.

In our experience most of our social workers have been brilliant. Some have fought with us. Most have fought for us. Once deemed the enemy, they are now friends and colleagues.

Paul could have said something similar about Christians. Once he thought of them as the enemy. He was so afraid of their beliefs leading people astray that he went to extreme lengths to eradicate them, murdering and threatening and persecuting them with a vengeance.

Then one night there was a seismic shift in his allegiance. Jesus himself stopped Paul in his tracks on his 140-mile journey to do damage to disciples in Damascus. There was a terrifying flash that blinded him. But he had seen the light. The Christians were not just spinning a tale. They were telling the truth. Jesus was now his Lord. Christians were now his friends and colleagues.

Paul the persecutor now identifies with the persecuted. He enters their atmosphere of fear. In the letter to the Romans he states how he left behind his world of prestige, status and power, and replaced it with suffering: trouble, hardship, persecution, famine, nakedness, damage, sword (Romans 8:35).

Why would he switch allegiances at such extreme cost? Look at how he explains it:

> For those who are led by the Spirit of God are the children of God. The Spirit you received does not make you slaves, so that you live in fear again; rather, the Spirit you received brought about your adoption to sonship. And by him we cry, '*Abba*, Father.' The Spirit himself testifies with our spirit that we are God's children. Now if we are children, then we are heirs – heirs of God and co-heirs with Christ, if indeed we share in his sufferings in order that we may also share in his glory. (Romans 8:14–17)

Paul uses the family structure of the ancient world to help us understand the incredible watershed that occurs when any of us become a Christian.

In the ancient world slaves were always second class, outsiders. They brushed shoulders each day with the family who had bought them. But they were never to think they belonged there.

New Testament scholar James Dunn explains: 'The idea of slavery . . . focuses on the slave's lack of freedom, as one who orders his life at another's behest, who must live within the terms of a code which restricts him firmly within servitude, and who as a slave is divided in status from members of the family by an unbridgeable gulf.'[1]

But what if this unbridgeable gulf could be bridged? What if outsiders can become insiders? What if strangers can become family? What if slaves can become sons and daughters?

There is something about the gospel that is implicit in every adoption. There is a mini-parable of the grace of God demonstrated every time a genuine adoption occurs. The outsider becomes the insider. The transient relationship becomes permanent. The fear factor is replaced by an intimate loving relationship.

The respected commentator F. F. Bruce points out that in the Roman world of the first century 'an adopted son was a son deliberately chosen by his adoptive father to perpetuate his name and inherit his estate; he was no whit inferior in status to a son born in the ordinary course of nature, and might well enjoy the father's affection more fully and reproduce the father's character more worthily'.[2]

What a transition. From affliction to affection. From outsider to insider. From servitude to security. From fear to family.

What are the fears we used to live in? Fear of death? Fear of not measuring up to other people's expectations? Fear of failure? Fear of letting someone down? Fear of getting caught out? Fear of financial ruin? Fear of the future? Perhaps those things still haunt us.

To us Paul says that the Holy Spirit in our life will remind us that we are adopted. When push comes to shove knowing that we have an eternal home in heaven with a Father who loves us makes even the most difficult situation a little more bearable.

My first day of secondary school was very stressful. Some of the boys decided to set fire to a car, and then panicked as the flames caught. In the absence of a fire extinguisher they decided to drop their trousers and try to urinate the flames out. What I saw that day should have prepared me for the year ahead. As I became the target of these crazy and cruel bullies, having a loving and secure home to go to at the end of the day was my lifeline.

Similarly, knowing now that I have a loving and secure home to go to when I die has helped me through many dark and fearful moments.

I remember one night in the docks, sitting with my wife on a suitcase under the stars while machine-gun fire cracked all around. We were waiting to be evacuated by the Italian navy, who, according to the BBC world service we were listening to on another evacuee's radio, had deemed the military situation in the country we were missionaries in too dangerous to intervene. That scared me.

I remember looking at the crash barriers of the motorway as I hurtled down at 70 mph and briefly thinking they looked more inviting than the office at work, where my employer was making allegations and threats. That scared me.

The antidote to fear is knowing that we belong some-where safe. This gives us hope, even in our darkest moments.

> We know that the whole creation has been groaning as in the pains of childbirth right up to the present time.

> Not only so, but we ourselves, who have the firstfruits of the Spirit, groan inwardly as we wait eagerly for our adoption to sonship, the redemption of our bodies. For in this hope we were saved. But hope that is seen is no hope at all. Who hopes for what they already have? But if we hope for what we do not yet have, we wait for it patiently. (Romans 8:22–25)

Hope. Hope. Hope. Hope. Hope. Paul can't say it often enough. Five times he repeats it in this short passage.

Our culture loves and longs for this kind of fear–hope turnaround.

The orphan-hero is a much-loved character in our films and literature. You can't miss it: Luke Skywalker, Batman, Spiderman, Superman, Harry Potter, Frodo Baggins, Dick Whittington, Pip from *Great Expectations*, Jane Eyre, Henry Fielding's Tom Jones, Remus and Romulus, Huckleberry Finn, Oliver Twist, Cinderella, Snow White, Mowgli, Paddington Bear, Tarzan – to name but a few. The idea of a foundling alone in the world who is taken in, fostered or adopted and then makes good is a dominant theme in many of our most-loved stories.

Why is this such a strong recurring theme?

Perhaps it has to do with the romantic rags-to-riches dream we tend to aspire to. Perhaps we all secretly want the underdog to win occasionally. Perhaps it is because being faced with vulnerable children we cannot help but become emotionally engaged. Perhaps the idea of being alone haunts us, and no one is quite as alone as an orphan.

Literary scholar Melanie Kimball argues: 'Orphan characters in folktales and literature symbolize our isolation from one another and from society. They do not belong to even the most basic of groups, the family unit, and in some cultures this is enough to cut them off from society at large . . . Orphans are a tangible reflection of the fear of abandonment that all humans experience.'[3]

The orphan-hero stories that fill our culture should inspire us and vulnerable children everywhere: change and hope and success and acceptance are possible, whatever our background. The real-life stories of orphan heroes even more so, for example journalist Kate Adie, model-turned-TV-chef Lorraine Pascale and footballer Mario Balotelli who show that their early experiences have not stopped them finding their potential.

Statistically, however, it is true that children in care are most likely to end up on the streets, in prisons and in refuges. There is a mismatch between the romantic notions on the silver screen and in our literature, and the stories we read in our newspapers.

What does come across loud and clear is that our culture is in search of hope. The hope that things could be better. The hope that in the world it is not just the strong who survive, or the rich who make good.

There is a hope that kindness, compassion and mercy could win out.

There is a deep-seated longing that abandonment, murder and malice need not have the last word.

There is a fascination with adoption, because it symbolises that possibility of turning deeply instilled fear to a life-changing hope. As Christians we have experienced this. We have the ultimate death-to-life, rags-to-riches story. We were lost and alone and now belong to an eternal family. We have seen that life is not about the survival of the fittest, but about the salvation of the most unlikely. We have lived in fear, and now we 'eagerly await our adoption' in great hope.

As we experience this with God, we can also illustrate it in our communities.

Here are two stories from different sides of the world with hopeful endings.

Jay was born afraid. Sometimes his mother was kind. Sometimes she would lock him in his room. Sometimes she would feed him. Sometimes she would attack him. This carried on for years. When a teacher noticed a bruise on his arm he was afraid, so he made up a story. He didn't know that she reported it anyway. There were other things that had made her suspicious. He had no friends. He was withdrawn. His attitude to school work lacked enthusiasm and pride.

A few months later when a burn matching the shape of an iron appeared, he was taken into care along with his siblings. After a few weeks he moved to a new foster home by himself, as someone felt that each of the children needed one-to-one help. Jay found it hard to trust his foster carer. The nicer she was, the more he expected her to flip into 'nasty' mode, and the more afraid he became. Months went by and just as he was beginning subconsciously to expect her kindness, he overheard a phone conversation. He was being put up for adoption. His worst fears had come true. She didn't really love him after all. She wanted shot of him just like his mother, who kept saying she would visit, but didn't.

Jay's adopters found themselves with a traumatised and fearful boy. It would take a lot of counselling and consistent care before Jay could express those fears. But soon after he did, he also began to talk about what he hoped for. It started off small. He wanted his new mum to watch him participate in assembly. He wanted to invite a friend over. He wanted to ride a horse. Jay's mum cried as he went off on his first pony trek camp some time later. A little hope had opened the door for Jay to give and receive love, to begin to enjoy his childhood, to discover his potential, safe in the knowledge he belonged somewhere for good.

On the other side of the world, Arya was chained to a table. Eight years old and never having attended school, he did not know life could be any different. He had dreams of running away, and had occasionally tried. He was afraid of what people could do to him, and was uncooperative and unfriendly to everyone.

When a local pastor heard about Arya he went to visit

his parents. He offered to help, and was told in no uncertain terms that this kid was a trouble-maker and not worth his time and effort. However, he persuaded them to hand over his care to some staff in his church. They were handed a fearful boy with terrible social skills and in need of some intensive help with his schooling.

After a while, somebody noticed that Arya had a natural sense of rhythm. One thing he had learned from his years of being chained to a table was the ability to tap out a beat and make music with his hands on the wood. They let him loose on a real drum kit, and invested in some music lessons.

Eight years later Arya still has difficulty in education and with socialising. But he regularly plays the drums in his local church. He leads worship with those hands that were chained.

Knowing that we have been adopted gives us hope instead of fear and gives us insight that enables us patiently to help frightened children like Jay and Arya.

Jay and Arya can also help us. Their stories give us insight into our relationship with God.

Sometimes we are like Arya, feeling like a failure by the world's standards, but holding in our hands a precious gift from the Father God who has always loved us and can redeem our worst experiences.

Sometimes we are like Jay, wrongly thinking that our adoptive Father God may suddenly turn on us, abandon us, disown us, not come through on his promises.

When will we learn that our adoptive Father God is not like that?

Paul really wants us to enjoy being loved by the God who chose us:

> If God is for us, who can be against us? He who did not spare his own Son, but gave him up for us all – how will he not also, along with him, graciously give us all things? Who will bring any charge against those whom God has chosen? It is God who justifies. Who then is the one who condemns? No one. Christ Jesus who died – more than that, who was raised to life – is at the right hand of God and is also interceding for us. Who shall separate us from the love of Christ? Shall trouble or hardship or persecution or famine or nakedness or danger or sword? As it is written:
>
> 'For your sake we face death all day long;
>
> we are considered as sheep to be slaughtered.'
>
> No, in all these things we are more than conquerors through him who loved us. For I am convinced that neither death nor life, neither angels nor demons, neither the present nor the future, nor any powers, neither height nor depth, nor anything else in all creation, will be able to separate us from the love of God that is in Christ Jesus our Lord. (Romans 8:31–39)

FOR FURTHER CONSIDERATION

How can we turn fear into hope for children around us? Think through the situations of these twelve children and how your family or your church could offer hope to them.

1. Alysha has Down's syndrome. Her carers' biggest fear is not whether she will live independently or not, but whether she will be treated well by the general public.

2. Dram is afraid to go to school. He feels different not only because he struggles academically but because he is adopted.

3. Jane is afraid of committing in any relationship. Her pattern is to be superficially nice if she can, and then to be manipulative and push people away.

4. Sally is afraid of men. Early experiences have made her extremely mistrustful, and although she can avoid them most of the time, it is hardest at the church she goes to where people give spontaneous hugs.

5. Rayan has an undiagnosed disability. He doesn't know how it will pan out and is afraid of the future.

6. Georgia's carers are besotted with their newly adopted baby, but she has a family history of

mental illness. They are afraid of what is around the corner.

7. Brook is nervous about trusting others. She has been let down many times and struggles with the effusive promises that she hears being made in church.

8. Ram is afraid of being seen as a failure. He disguises it most of the time. On the football field he keeps lashing out, although it is a sport in which he seems to have a natural flair.

9. Torqui is afraid of everyone. Painfully shy, he prefers to be left alone.

10. Jacky is afraid of not being loved. She has gone through a string of inappropriate relationships and is currently in with a guy who takes hard drugs.

11. Sophie and Sammy are afraid that when they leave foster care, they will end up in separate adoptive families. They wonder how they will cope without the other one there and if they will ever see each other again.

CLAIRE'S STORY

We are a family with four great children, our youngest, Isabelle, is adopted. Isabelle was placed with us in July 2009 at fourteen months and because of a chromosomal disorder has some physical and learning difficulties as well as some medical issues.

My husband and I started this journey in 2007 and from the outset had decided to adopt a child with some disabilities. Having both had twenty years' experience working with children, including those with a level of disability, we felt we could take on a child with additional needs.

Our journey was quite a roller coaster! We went to approval panel twice, eventually being approved in 2009, and then after a six-month journey intending to adopt a little girl with cerebral palsy the Local Authority pulled out just before matching panel. If we had not firmly believed that this was what God was calling us to and put our hope and trust in him we could easily have given up. God was and is our strength.

After getting over all these difficult times, in April 2009 we were given the details of Isabelle. We were tentative and tried to protect ourselves but we couldn't get her out of our minds. She was a lovely little 11-month-old with a beautiful smile but with significant developmental delay, and because of family background she was expected to have a learning disability. We knew in our hearts that she was right for us and couldn't believe that we could adopt this wonderful child. The process began and with no hold-ups or problems we went to matching panel three months later and within days we took her home forever. We could not have predicted how well she has fitted into our family. Everyone has adored her from the moment she arrived.

As time has gone by the petals of our 'little flower' have gradually opened and we are discovering more of the extent of her disabilities but also more of her beautiful, loving, caring and empathetic heart. She can be difficult at times and we spend a lot of time at hospital appointments and fighting for what she needs, but she is so worth it. Despite her needs she has been a real blessing to our family and to our church's life. We have been amazed too at how our older birth children have nurtured and cared for their little sister.

God is glorified in Isabelle's life, in her smile, in the way she 'dances' and 'sings' (loudly!) in church and we are very privileged to be the parents of this very special little girl. Adopting and living with a child with disabilities can sometimes be hard but we definitely feel we are the ones who are blessed!

CHAPTER 10

WHY HARD-TO-PLACE CHILDREN CAN FIND A HOME FOR GOOD

When I was a teenager my friend Lucy was told by her birth mother that she was an accident and that she wished she had aborted her.

Just a few words, but they cut through this young girl like a knife. They sliced into her self-esteem, her self-image and her sense of self-worth. She felt lost. Home just wasn't home for her any more.

She fell into a depression and attempted suicide on numerous occasions. She felt she had no reason to live because she felt no one in the world wanted her. It was so hard to watch the disintegration of a young woman. I prayed as hard as I ever had and did my best to explain to her, as best I could at sixteen, that her birth mother was only part of the story, that God had knit her together in her mother's womb, that for God there was no such thing as an unplanned pregnancy – that for God there are no unwanted children.

There are many, many kids around who feel, like Lucy, that nobody loves them, and nobody wants them. Lots of them are on the adoption 'waiting list'.

Approved adopters can use family-finding services to explore potential matches with children who are waiting. These services tend to profile children in a national forum, when local authorities and agencies have been unable to find adopters locally. One of these, the website 'Link Maker', featured more than 3,000 children last year. Most of them were white children aged between two and ten years old, many had specified additional needs and more than half of them were looking for a new home along with their sibling or siblings.

Websites like this are torturous to look through. There is picture after picture of happy, smiling children, and then a brief heartbreaking description of each of them recounted below.

When Zoe was looking to adopt her first child, she used a family-finding magazine, which she found very overwhelming. How could she possibly choose a child to welcome into her home? Just glancing at the pictures brought tears to her eyes as she felt the weight of the responsibility. Her young niece couldn't read but found a picture in the magazine. 'I like this one,' she said pointing. Zoe made an enquiry and a few months later Amber became her daughter. To anyone who didn't know, they would never have guessed that Amber was adopted. She had a similar temperament to her mum, the same gentle smile, and the same skin tone. A few years later Zoe's two nephews were taken into care. Zoe knew she had to fight to be a mother for them too, but it was never going to be an easy journey. It cost her her marriage.

If it is hard for us to stomach those family-finding profiles, how much harder must it be for the children? What must go through their minds as they wait for a family month after month? At what age do the children understand that prospective adopters are browsing a website or reading through profiles and passing them by? Are their stories not interesting enough, their smiles not wide enough, their medical histories not clean enough, their behaviours not good enough, their faces not young enough for what prospective adopters are looking for?

Thinking that you don't measure up or may get left on the shelf as your childhood passes – what does that do to an already fragile young heart? Does it slice through them like a knife, shredding their self-esteem and self-worth to ribbons like my friend Lucy experienced?

Some of them know that their birth parents don't want them any more. Some of them know that their birth parents want them but they want their drugs or their alcohol more. Some of them have no idea about their birth parents and wonder if anyone will ever love them.

How I wish we could let these children know that for God there is no such thing as an unplanned pregnancy, that for God there are no unwanted children.

Here's another story, another woman who felt unwanted.

Dee bravely told her moving life story while she stood waist deep in a birthing pool doubling up for a makeshift baptistery. Her father's violence and mother's indifference led her to run away from home at the age of fifteen when she ended up living on the streets. During her adult life she had lost children both to the care system and through bereavement, and felt like God and the world were against her. When her youngest son began to come to Sunday school, she discovered a group of people who welcomed, accepted and loved her just the way she was. There wasn't a dry eye in the room as she explained that coming to know Jesus had transformed her life and made her feel special for the first time. Then she was soaked in water to rapturous applause.

Dee's story of God breaking into her life two years ago is powerful. But actually God broke into her life way before then – millennia of years earlier. When God created the world he picked her out as his adopted daughter-to-be. She was never an unwanted child.

When Paul writes to the Gentile Christians in the letter to the Ephesians, he starts off with this assurance that God has no unwanted children.

> Praise be to the God and Father of our Lord Jesus Christ, who has blessed us in the heavenly realms with every spiritual blessing in Christ. For he chose us in him before the creation of the world to be holy and blameless in his sight. In love he predestined us for adoption to sonship through Jesus Christ, in accordance with his pleasure and will – to the praise of his glorious grace. (Ephesians 1:3–6)

Paul is writing to the non-Jewish Christians in the early Church who often struggled with feeling like they didn't really belong in God's family. They did not have the Jewish heritage, traditions and Temple. They were not familiar with the law or with circumcision. They were in the minority, and not always accepted by the Jewish Christians. Nor, as followers of God, did they fit in with the Gentile culture around them either, with their multiple gods and cult worship and their practice of magic. Everywhere they turned they felt unwanted.

Paul reassures them by reminding them that the story for all Christians starts way back before the creation of the universe. God chose us before we were born, in fact before the universe itself was birthed.

Before the big bang. Before the galaxies were formed. Before our solar system existed. Before God scattered the constellations or created DNA.

Even way back then God had in mind to adopt us. Human rebellion did not take God by surprise. Jesus' sacrificial death for us was not plan B because we messed up his plan A. It was not a gross miscarriage of justice that God had to come and fix by raising Jesus from the dead. The creation, the cross, the resurrection were all premeditated so that you and I could be adopted into God's family.

Is it possible that many Christians still feel insecure, detached, lacking in hope and purpose precisely because this image has been neglected in our churches?

Is it possible that many Christians still feel like 'spiritual orphans' because they have been insufficiently taught about their status as adopted children?

Is it possible that many children are still feeling unwanted, waiting for adoption because we haven't understood the powerful image of adoption that is painted in Ephesians?

Dan Cruver, an American author and adoptive father passionate about orphan care worldwide, suggested to me that the reason that fostering and adoption is not higher up the Church's agenda is that most Christians have failed to grasp the significance and privilege of being adopted into God's family. He writes: 'Adoption was not a divine afterthought. It was in God's triune mind and heart before the first tick of human history's clock. Adoption therefore predates the universe itself. Only God and his triune love are "bigger" than adoption.'[1]

Dan Cruver teaches that this 'vertical' experience of our adoption by God must have a knock-on effect that impacts a 'horizontal' experience of adopting kids who are waiting.

Adoption is the big secret of the universe. It is the central idea among a whole list that Paul wraps up into a prayer for a church of ordinary people in Ephesus who had a tendency to feel insecure. Jews, Gentiles, men and women and children, slaves, free people – all of them are included in God's adoption plans. None of them is an accident. None of their births were biological mishaps. None of their ethnic backgrounds or social positions exclude them from experiencing the highest privilege it is possible for a human being to receive: adoption into the household of the King of kings.

All this was planned before the sun ever rose over the earth, before pulsars beat the celestial rhythm of the universe, before tectonic plates shifted, before the Ice Age, before the first breath was taken.

You have to admire the patience of God. Billions of years in eternity past God planned this, but it is only now beginning to crescendo. Talk about seeing the bigger picture. Talk about attention to detail.

But if God can order billions of minute details of the universe such that Jesus' birth can perfectly match prophecies made centuries earlier, then why does he seem to get other births all wrong? Parents like Lucy's fall pregnant by accident and struggle to love their children, while other couples would love to have children but just can't get pregnant. Why do people who can't care for their own children and often don't want the children they have got find it so easy to conceive, and yet others who desperately want children and are willing to go to great lengths, great expense and through great heartache just can't? It seems unfair. It seems like God's perfect planning has a huge glitch.

Sometimes the Bible seems to rub salt into the wound for childless couples. It seems like everyone in the Bible who is mentioned as barren ends up miraculously getting pregnant eventually. There's Abraham and Sarah (Genesis 11), Rebekah and Isaac (Genesis 25), Jacob and Rachel (Genesis 29), Manoah and Zorah (Judges 13), Hannah and Elkanah (1 Samuel 1), Elizabeth and Zechariah (Luke 1). Six out of six women end up giving birth to a child.

The first thing to say is that these six childless couples are not typical. The fact that God intervened miraculously ensured that their stories were remembered. Just because every leper mentioned in the New Testament got healed did not mean that every leper in Jesus' day got healed. Similarly these families are not representative of every barren couple. Their inclusion implies countless other barren couples for whom there was no miraculous conception.

These six stories of God's miraculous intervention are also atypical because they each introduce a major player in salvation history: Isaac, Jacob, Joseph, Samson, Samuel and John the Baptist.

God deliberately chose an elderly barren couple to launch Israel the nation, and he sustained that nation by sending them patriarchs and prophets who were supernaturally born. The very birth and existence of the nation of Israel was a miracle both physically and spiritually.

God has a habit of taking despairing couples and using the thing they struggle with most to show something amazing to the world.

There is no glitch in the system. God is underlining that he is very much in control.

Like so many other forms of suffering and injustice, we may only ever understand what God is doing when we look back on life from the vantage point of centuries of history, even from eternity.

I remember sitting with my wife after our second

miscarriage wondering what was going on. Wondering what to say to comfort and console her. Wondering about those families in our church with six and seven children and what they had done to deserve such an easy ride. Wanting to avoid our church weekend away. Feeling unable to go to church because I didn't know how to talk about what we were experiencing.

And I was the pastor.

How could I help other families in the same boat when I couldn't come to terms with our own loss?

Conception and pregnancy felt like our only option to grow our family as we had already approached several fostering and adoption services and been put off by people on the phone. Looking back perhaps we weren't trusting in God's call or God's timing. Perhaps he knew we weren't yet ready. Somehow out of those painful experiences, God worked things out for the good. Without them our family would never have experienced the joys and fulfilment that have come from fostering and adopting.

Adoption and fostering are not God's back-up plan. Adoption is not the last resort for couples who really want to work their families out naturally. Adoption is not the last resort for the children who naturally really want it to work out with their birth families.

Adoption is God's first choice.

When James and Donna got married, they decided they would grow their family through adoption. They still have no idea if they could have children naturally or not. They don't care. They felt called in this way to live out the truth that adoption is God's plan A.

This is not for everyone. And not all barren couples will be called or able to foster or adopt. There may be other purposes to that terrible pain that will only be revealed in the light of eternity. Childlessness, like singleness, was the path chosen by Jesus as he lived on earth, and he was the most perfect human being that has ever lived, so nobody should be made to feel guilty for embracing either childlessness or singleness.

The parallel issues of unwanted childlessness and 'unwanted children' are no accident. Could these twin pains be God's means of grace? Grace to us as parents? Grace to vulnerable children? Grace to the world we live in?

God, who sees the pain and knows what it is like to lose an only child, says that there are no unplanned pregnancies, no unwanted children. There are more ways to be family than genetic connections. Love trumps biology.

How can we let the thousands of children in care waiting for adoption know that they are not unwanted children? That they won't be left parentless because of their additional needs, their siblings, their age, their history?

Instead of leaving them to wait and wonder if they will be left on the shelf, how would they feel if they knew people were queuing up to adopt them?

Some children get adopted quickly, usually the younger, nicer-looking ones meeting their developmental milestones and with no complications on their family medical history.

Everyone else is placed into a category called 'hard-to-place' kids. These include sibling groups, older children, children of black and ethnic minority families and children with complex special needs, including disabilities, trauma and the effects of extreme abuse.

Imagine if there were Christians queuing up to offer hard-to-place children a home for good. Childless couples, larger families, single adopters – male and female. Grandparents. Blended families. Families who want to use their home for God by offering vulnerable children a home for good. Families who want the world to know – there are no unwanted children.

FOR FURTHER CONSIDERATION

You have reached the end of the book. We hope this is the start of a new journey for you. Work through the questions below and make some of those life-changing decisions today.

1. Will you help make fostering and adoption a priority in your church? How?
2. Will you offer real, practical and reliable help and support to those in your church or your community who are fostering or adopting children? How?
3. Would you be willing to offer yourselves as

emergency or respite foster carers? What will you do to get the ball rolling?

4. Would you be willing to offer yourselves as short-term or long-term foster carers? What will you do to get the ball rolling?

5. Would you be willing to adopt a child? What will you do to get the ball rolling?

6. Would you be willing to adopt a sibling group? What will you do to get the ball rolling?

7. Would you be willing to adopt a child with additional needs? What will you do to get the ball rolling?

8. Would you be willing to help children find their spiritual home for good? How?

9. Would you be willing to make helping vulnerable children a key value in your occupation? How?

10. What other skills or resources do you have that could benefit the poor and vulnerable in your community?

SHEGUN'S STORY

When my wife first suggested adoption to me, I would not have any of it. I believe it was due to the fact that I felt adoption was not the answer to our childlessness. I guess I was a bit selfish. My wife had been diagnosed with polycystic ovaries. I felt the medical cause of our childlessness was not my fault. I thought we could look at surrogacy. At least the child would be my blood.

A chance conversation made the difference. As a Christian, I believe everything happens for a reason. I asked God to show me beyond a shadow of doubt if adoption was something he wanted us to do. And show me he did!

Our adopted son came into our lives. We gave him all the love we had. He reciprocated over and above what we ever expected. And to my surprise we had a lot of love left for the birth children who came along in due course. And there appears to be more in store if God says we will have more children.

I can say hand on heart that the love I have for our adopted son is no different from the love I have for our birth children. I love all three dearly and there is no difference.

Shegun Olusanya runs an event management company with his wife and have been shortlisted as Adoption Champion of the Year at the National Adoption Week Awards.

CHAPTER 11

WHAT NEXT?

The cops are coming. We have a reliable source that tells us in twenty minutes the squad car will enter our road. Twelve hundred seconds to sort everything out. Stuff needs to be hidden. Furniture needs to be rearranged. Someone needs to grab supplies from the loft.

But this is no raid. Two children have been found abandoned in their home. Two children have spent fretful hours and hours in police custody. They are not even five years old. And they need a bed for one night so the parents can be located and helped.

The foster carers want to make sure these children don't just get a bed for the night. They want to make sure they get a warm welcome, a place that feels safe and homely. Pyjamas of the right ages are located. Barbie duvets are replaced with Thomas the Tank Engine ones. Familiar food is prepared. Diaries are cleared.

It is not rocket science. It is stuff anyone could do. Twenty minutes to make a huge difference to those children's first experience of foster care and begin to communicate that eternal truth – for God there are no unwanted children.

We hope we have made two things clear to you through this book.

First, caring for the poor, the marginalised, the widows and the orphans is a basic and essential part of Christian discipleship. It is not for keen or mature or elite Christians, it is not for far lefty political types or mansion dwellers or unemployed youth workers. It is a basic aspect of what God expects of all of his followers. He wants to be known as a father to the fatherless and a protector of widows and orphans. Then we who know the joy and privilege of being adopted into his family need to join God's family business.

Second, there are vulnerable children waiting for foster and adoptive homes, waiting right here on our doorstep in the UK, and the Church is ideally placed to help meet the need – some Christians to wrap around those children by offering them a home for good, everyone else to wrap around those Christians to ensure their stability and stick-ability, and all of us together to be one big foster family, one big adopted family.

I used to imagine being there with Corrie Ten Boom during the Nazi occupation of Holland, risking everything to shelter Jews as they were hunted down by the Nazis.

I used to imagine being there with William Wilberforce, giving time and talent and a political career to champion the cause of kidnapped Africans who were being sold as slaves in the transatlantic slave trade.

I used to imagine being there with Gladys Aylwood, rescuing Chinese orphans from the attacks of Japanese soldiers and bomber aircraft, and travelling a hundred miles by foot despite suffering from typhus and pneumonia.

It is easy to romanticise. Now is our time. Who will step up to find and rescue and love the thousands of children waiting for a home for good?

AFTERWORD

Thank you for reading the home for good book. Can we journey with you as you explore what's next? Home for Good is passionate about equipping and supporting individuals, families and churches to respond to the needs of vulnerable children. There is so much that we can do that will make a difference. By exploring fostering or adoption, by being part of the supportive community around fostering and adopting families, or by raising awareness and advocating on behalf of vulnerable children, you can be part of ensuring that every child has a safe, secure and loving home for good. We believe that everybody has a part to play and we would love to help you consider what yours might be.

Has the book inspired you to consider caring directly for vulnerable children through fostering or adoption? We would love to talk this through, answer your questions and pray for you as you start this journey. Call the Home for Good team on 0300 001 0995 or make an enquiry through our website, which is also full of stories and information about the joys and challenges of fostering and adoption, and gives you details of the application and assessment process.

Has the book prompted you to offer more support to families who care for vulnerable children? We would love to equip you to do this and our website is packed with resources and ideas to enable you. Being part of a supportive community could make all the difference for a family facing challenges, and the more people who can wrap around them with care and practical support the better. Perhaps you could give this book to someone else to read so that they too will be inspired to help.

Has the book challenged you to raise more awareness of the needs of vulnerable children? We know that not everyone can foster or adopt, or it may not be something you can do right now, but you can still make a difference in the lives of children who have experienced the care system. You could use our resources to inform your church, add your voice to our advocacy campaigns, or raise money to enable Home for Good to do even more. Our website has all the information you will need to respond to the need in the way that you are called to.

Whatever your next step might be, Home for Good is keen to walk with you on the journey. Together, we can find a home for every child who needs one.

www.homeforgood.org.uk

ACKNOWLEDGEMENTS

Our heartfelt thanks to all the following people who have shaped and re-shaped this book.

To all at Hodder, especially Ian Metcalfe, Joanna Davey and Hannah Ward.

To our script-readers for your suggestions and encouragements, including Rob Parsons, Nicky Gumbel, Patrick Regan, Steve Holmes, Steve Clifford, Dan Cruver, Keith Brown, Sue Colman, Jedd Medefind, Lois Putt, Sally Hobson, Steve Morris and Charis Gibson.

To Mark Molden and Steve Williams for your excitement at the conception of all that *Home for Good* will be.

To the contributors for your stories which are at the heart of the book: Ashley Jean Baptiste, Diane Louise Jordan, Jason Kovaks, Claire and Alan Charter, Sam Ursell, Miranda Heathcote, Elizabeth Thomas, Tara Bradford, Andy Reed, Rachel and Jason Gardner, Arianne Winslow, Simon and Marianne Langley, Viv Thomas, Shegun Olusanya, 'Gran and Grandad', and David Hennessey.

To the fantastic social workers who have worked with us this year, especially Gill Evans, Rachel Dunbar and Eleanor Bartlett, Jan Fishwick from PACT and Jane Elston at BAAF who has helped with statistics.

To all at Cornerstone Church for your day-to-day support and for caring with us for children who come through our homes.

To Rachel and Paul Hill who helped us have a holiday this year.

To all the other local adopters and foster carers who have shared lives with us.

To our forever children, Joel, Luke, Anna and Elly, who are the most amazing young foster carers we have ever met. Thank you for accepting each new arrival into your lives with patience, compassion and a sense of humour.

To our foster children, past, present and future. Your names are written on our hearts. Even though you may have been with us only temporarily, each of you has blessed our home for good.

NOTES

INTRODUCTION

1. See the Christian Alliance for Orphans' White Paper on Understanding Orphan Statistics: www.cafo.org/wp-content/uploads/2015/10/Orphan-Statistics-Web-9-2015.pdf

2. National statistics on 'Children looked after in England, year ending 31 March 2018' were released by the Department for Education on 15 November 2018 according to the arrangements approved by the UK statistics authority: www.gov.uk/government/statistics/children-looked-after-in-england-including-adoption-2017-to-2018.

CHAPTER 1

1. L. Ryken, J. Wilhoit, T. Longman, C. Duriez, D. Penney and D. G. Reid, *Dictionary of Biblical Imagery* (InterVarsity Press, 2000), electronic ed., p. 615.

2. NSPCC annual summary: www.nspcc.org.uk/Inform/research/statistics/child_protection_register_statistics_wda48723.html

3. See www.homeforgood.org.uk/statistics

4. See the Fostering Network recruitment targets: www.thefosteringnetwork.org.uk/advice-information/all-about-fostering/recruitment-targets.

5. Jason Kovacs is co-founder of Together for Adoption and Director of Ministry Development for the ABBA Fund.

CHAPTER 2

1. Sue Gerhardt, *Why Love Matters. How Affection Shapes a Baby's Brain* (Routledge, 2004), p. 218.

2. R. A. Cole, *Exodus: An Introduction and Commentary*, Tyndale Old Testament Commentaries, vol. 2 (Inter-Varsity Press, 1973), electronic ed., p. 64.

3. The word 'basket' (*teba*) is the same as 'ark' in Genesis 6 – 9; 'papyrus' (*gome*) is a different word. (The word is probably borrowed from an Egyptian word, *tbt*, meaning something like 'square box' or even 'coffin'.) Moses was placed in a *teba gome*, a 'papyrus coffin'; Noah sailed in a *teba* made of 'atsey gopher' – gopher wood.

4. Adoption UK report, 'It Takes a Village to Raise a Child', March 2012.

5. See Helen Oakwater, *Bubble Wrapped Children* (MX Publishing, 2012), p. 30.

CHAPTER 3

1. *Rabbit-Proof Fence*, directed by Philip Noyce, 2002.

2. Kate Adie, *Nobody's Child: Who Are You When You Don't Know Your Past?* (Hodder, 2005), p. 7.

3. See Helen Oakwater, *Bubble Wrapped Children* (MX Publishing, 2012).

4. Rachel Gardner is Director of Youthscape, Founder of Romance Academy, author and speaker. Jason Gardner is a curate with 20 years of youth ministry experience.

CHAPTER 4

1. Numbers 10:35.

2. Perhaps George Lucas and Steven Spielberg were thinking of verse 2 of this psalm when they directed the climactic scene of *Raiders of the Lost Ark*, as the Nazis melted like wax before the fire.

3. 2 Samuel 9.

4. 1 Samuel 13:14 and Acts 13:22.

CHAPTER 5

1. Albert Camus, *The Plague* (Penguin Modern Classics, 2002).

2. Fyodor Dostoyevsky, *The Brothers Karamazov* (Penguin, 1983).

3. Mary Beth Chapman, *Choosing to See: A Journey of Struggle and Hope* (Revell, 2010).

4. Ibid, p. 256.

5. Jayne E. Schooler et al., *Wounded Children, Healing Homes: How Traumatized Children Impact Adoptive and Foster Families* (NavPress, 2010).

6. At 11.35 a.m. on 3 August 2007, an ambulance was called

to the house. Its crew found Baby P already stiff and blue in his blood-spattered cot. As they tried to rush him to hospital, the mother demanded they wait while she collected her cigarettes. See www.guardian.co.uk/society/2008/nov/12/child-protection-crime-baby-p

7. Helen Oakwater, *Bubble Wrapped Children* (MX Publishing, 2012), pp. 37ff.

8. Ibid., pp. 97ff.

9. Schooler, *Wounded Children, Healing Homes*, p. 27.

CHAPTER 6

1. Dr Viv Thomas is the founder and Director of Formation, an organisation set up to provide teaching and mentoring for Christian leaders. Among other things he is also the Honorary Teaching Pastor at St Paul's Hammersmith, an ordained Anglican, an Associate Lecturer at Spurgeon's College, London, an organisational consultant and a writer.

2. http://www.bcministry.net

CHAPTER 7

1. Elizabeth Thomas is part of Manna, a charity working to see the Anglican church in Mozambique and Angola growing and thriving.

CHAPTER 8

1. www.huffingtonpost.com/tamar-abrams/artyom-savelyev-to-russia_b_532621.html

2. See Lesley Ashmall and Mario Cacciottolo, `I sent my

adopted son back into care', BBC News, January 2017, www.bbc.co.uk/news/uk-38764302

3. Melanie Allen, *The Trouble with Alex* (Pocket Books, 2009).

4. John 13:1.

CHAPTER 9

1. J. D. G. Dunn, *Romans 1 – 8*, Word Biblical Commentary, vol. 38A (Word Inc., 1998), electronic ed., p. 460.

2. F. F. Bruce, *Romans: An Introduction and Commentary*, Tyndale New Testament Commentaries, vol. 6 (InterVarsity Press, 1985), electronic ed., p. 167.

3. Melanie A. Kimball, 'From Folk Tales to Fiction: Orphan Characters in Children's Literature', *Library Trends*, vol. 47, no. 3 (Winter 1999), pp. 558–78.

CHAPTER 10

1. Dan Cruver (ed.), *Reclaiming Adoption: Missional Living through the Rediscovery of Abba Father* (Cruciform Press, 2011), p. 12.

HODDER &
STOUGHTON

Hodder & Stoughton is the UK's
leading Christian publisher,
with a wide range of books from
the bestselling authors in the UK
and around the world ranging from
Christian lifestyle and theology to
apologetics, testimony and fiction.
We also publish the world's
most popular Bible translation
in modern English, the New
International Version, renowned
for its accuracy and readability.

Hodderfaith.com   Hodderbibles.co.uk
@HodderFaith   /HodderFaith